CO

ISBN: 983 - 9312 - 01 - 4

Published & Distributed by:-
Sabah Handicraft Centre
Lot 1, Pusat Perindustrian Kolombong Jaya,
Mile 5 1/2, Jalan Kolombong,
88450 Kota Kinabalu, Sabah, Malaysia.
Tel./Fax: 60-88-438309
Email: catherine@borneoecotours.com

For tour information, please contact :-
Albert C.K.Teo
Managing Director
Borneo Eco Tours Sdn. Bhd.
Lot 1, Pusat Perindustrian Kolombong Jaya,
Mile 5 1/2, Jalan Kolombong,
88450 Kota Kinabalu, Sabah, Malaysia.
Tel: 60-88-438300   Fax: 60-88-438307
Email: info@borneoecotours.com
Website: www.borneoecotours.com

Cover: *Face of a proboscis monkey*
Photo by Albert C.K. Teo

Foreword

Developing tourism in any region requires careful planning. A variety of issues need to be considered. Among them are local community values and needs. Policies are also needed to encourage appropriate development, supported by legislation to ensure the environment and resources are suitably protected. The State Government will continue to take a leadership role in developing an enduring tourism industry, but our efforts are made much easier where private businesses join with government, conservation groups, and communities to achieve sustainability goals.

Two of our supporters in reaching these goals have been Sukau Rainforest Lodge and Borneo Eco Tours, tireless promoters of ecotourism. These organizations, and their founder, Albert Teo, share a vision for Borneo that includes viewing opportunities of its unique wildlife and where the people who live in these rare and fragile environments are able to enjoy a livelihood that is in harmony with its sensitive nature.

The book **Saving Paradise: The Story of Sukau Rainforest Lodge** illustrates how a tourism business can balance environment concerns with the need to make a profit. We have been given a rare insight to the trials and tribulations involved in developing a working ecolodge. This book is not an academic discussion of the possibilities and pitfalls of ecotourism, but instead a real-life case study of how ecotourism principles can be applied with success.

Sabah offers some of the world's greatest treasures for nature lovers and travelers. A trip here can provide lifetime memories as people watch wildlife, hike, raft, dive or sight-see. Towards this end we would like to ensure that these activities continue for visitor enjoyment as well as to generate local economic benefits through appropriate development of supporting infrastructure. I believe many people will enjoy the beautiful photographs of **Saving Paradise: The Story of Sukau Rainforest Lodge**, and at the same time I hope also that they will learn from the lessons the book offers to ensure that they travel with care in this special place.

(TAN SRI DATUK CHONG KAH KIAT)
Deputy Chief Minister / Minister of Tourism, Culture and Environment
Sabah, Malaysia
January 2005

Dedication

This book is dedicated to
KARI BIN ONGONG
**the one man who had the courage to step out
of his comfort zone to provide a livelihood for his people.**

Kari (right) poses with Albert Teo in front of the Lodge (2003)

Message

The floodplain of the Lower Kinabatangan River is a key site for conservation of the natural environment. It is one of Malaysia's largest floodplains, special and rare, providing economic opportunities to the inhabitants, acting as a water filtering system to the environment and a source of water to the people of Sandakan. It is home to many rare and endangered species and thus the heritage and livelihood of the people.

The Lower Kinabatangan is highlighted as an ecotourism 'hotspot' in the National Ecotourism Plan and the Sabah Tourism Master Plan. It is special because it offers one of the best wildlife viewing location and freshwater swamp rain forest in Southeast Asia. It has been declared a Wildlife Sanctuary by the Sabah state government for which one of the main reasons cited was for the potential of tourism for job creation and economic growth among the local communities. In Malaysia the government encourages the growth of ecotourism because when responsibly practised it allows the preservation of our heritage making tourism and conservation acceptable.

The Lower Kinabatangan Wildlife Sanctuary is Malaysia's first Gift To The Earth, a commitment by the Sabah state government in November 1999 to conserve the area for its vast biodiversity and tourism value that is being complemented by a Vision 'Kinabatangan, A Corridor of Life ' launched in January 2002 in collaboration with WWF Partners for Wetlands Programme for a forest corridor along the Kinabatangan connecting the coastal mangrove swamps with the upland forests, where people, wildlife, nature-based tourism and local agricultural industries thrive and support each other.

The Sukau Rainforest Lodge spearheaded by Albert Teo is a model ecolodge which is in line with the Sabah state government ecotourism objective and with WWF Partners For Wetlands Vision for Ecotourism Development in the Lower Kinabatangan Floodplains, tourism will further benefit through a shared vision of an ideal development scenario. The development of tourism has to be a sustainable and responsible economic activity in active partnership with local communities, supporting the preservation of habitat and biodiversity through the code of best practices and the Wildlife Sanctuary Management Plan, using natural resources in a sustainable way, minimizing consumption, waste and pollution, respecting local culture, ensuring local communities benefit from tourism development and educating staff, overseas counterpart and tourists on conservation.

Saving Paradise – The Story of Sukau Rainforest Lodge is a road map to further understand and appreciate the challenges and the way forward to sustainable ecotourism development.

Albert Teo must be congratulated in producing this book and the many international eco awards given to his brainchild the Sukau Rainforest Lodge.

Tengku Datuk (Dr) Zainal Adlin
Chairman
Sabah Tourism Board / WWF Malaysia

Tourists on the scenic boatride from Sandakan to Sukau

A female Proboscis monkey

Saving Paradise
The Story of Sukau Rainforest Lodge

The constant chatter of the insects on the night shift had started to fade and the neighbor's cat that had been looking for love in all the wrong places had decided to turn in. The soft hoot of the gibbons was my next clue that daybreak was approaching. I stretched on the bed and wiggled my toes, enjoying the feel of the moist tropical air on my skin. I watched a gecko do a final patrol of the ceiling looking for his next meal. My stomach rumbled, reminding me that it was almost time for my next meal, a selection of savory Malaysian dishes. A kingfisher called in the distance and I heard the voices of the men along the river readying the boats for the day's trips. Soft footsteps sounded on the walkway outside my window as someone slipped in some early bird watching. I thought of the morning boat ride yet to come, wondering if today we would be lucky enough to spot the elusive Pygmy elephants. Someone knocked softly at the door marking the official start of another day at Sukau. It was time to get up and begin another period of fascinating exploration that is so typical of time spent in the Kinabatangan River basin.

This was the beginning of my day at the Sukau Rainforest Lodge in October 2002. I've returned since then to enjoy the riches of the Kinabatangan River area and I find the story of how this lodge came to be as interesting as the wildlife one can see while visiting it.

The lodge was the brainchild of Albert Teo, President and Founder of Borneo Eco Tours. As Albert observed "an ecotourism tour without a lodge is not complete". So he undertook to build a lodge that would provide great wildlife watching experiences and become a base of operations for the Kinabatangan area while also demonstrating sustainable building and operating principles. His vision also included a meaningful role for the people living in the Sukau area.

This book tells the story of the Sukau Rainforest Lodge. It tells in Albert's words how it was built, how it is operated and why it continues to succeed when many ecotourism facilities struggle. It is also a story of the Kinabatangan River basin, an area of incredible biotic diversity and of the Orang Sungai people who have lived closely with this river for many hundreds of years.

Despite his great accomplishments, Albert remains a humble man. He is very quick to give credit to and share his success with others who have helped along the way. Throughout this book. his name is prominent; but Albert would like the readers to know that the accomplishments are not his alone. He readily shares credit with Lodge management, supporters and backers. Where you see his name in this book, remember there is a legion of people behind him.

The Sukau Rainforest Lodge has lessons for the tourism industry, not just for other organizations wanting to create an ecolodge. It has lessons for travelers who seldom wonder about the infrastructure that goes into delivering a rich vacation experience far into the rainforest. This book shares these lessons with the hope that others will gain insights and work together to protect ecosystems through responsible travel.

Enjoy.

Carol Patterson

Ashy Tailorbird

Why an Ecolodge?

To understand Albert Teo's desire to build a lodge that balances conservation and economic interests, you must first learn something about the Kinabatangan River and the region that eco-adventurers call the mini Amazon.

The Sukau Rainforest Lodge is perched on the banks of one of Asia's most important waterways, the Kinabatangan River in the eastern Malaysian state of Sabah on the island of Borneo. To reach the Lodge, one must take a two-hour boat ride from the city of Sandakan on the eastern coast of Sabah or make a 130 kilometer trip overland. The Lodge's nearest neighbors are found in the village of Sukau, 10 minutes downriver by boat.

Sukau is a small community of 1,000 people who have depended on the Kinabatangan River for their livelihood for many generations. The original people in this area are the *Orang Sungai* or the River People. They share close cultural and spiritual connections with the Kinabatangan River which serves as a source of food and drinking water, provides a place for daily bathing and hygiene, and is an important transportation route.

At 560 kilometers, the Kinabatangan River is Sabah's longest river. Although visually it is indistinguishable from many meandering, silt-colored waterways in Southeast Asia, the floodplain of the Kinabatangan is one of the most exceptional areas in eastern Malaysia, sometimes carrying the title of the "mini-Amazon".

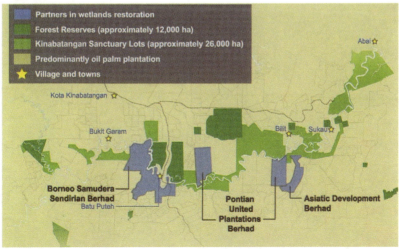

Oriental darter

Pygmy elephants feeding by the bank of the Kinabatangan River

Squirrel

Monitor lizard

Mangrove tree snake

Longtailed macaque

Silver langur

Reticulated python

Bearded pig and piglets feeding on figs

The lower part of the river plain floods regularly due to the heavy rainfalls and the influence of the Sulu Sea. As a result there are five distinct habitats found in the lower Kinabatangan river basin: waterlogged and dry forests, saline and freshwater swamps, and limestone forests. This range of habitats produces an amazing diversity of wildlife. In the lower Kinabatangan it is possible to see 10 primate species including the Proboscis monkey, the Orang-utan, and the Bornean gibbon. Among the 50 recorded mammals species found here are the Pygmy Elephant and the bearded pig. There are more than 200 bird species and more than 1500 plant species including the newly discovered *Ceriscoides "kinabatangensis"*, a pod-bearing tree unique to Borneo.

> *"I think Sabah is still the nucleus of the biodiversity of the world, especially when the Orang-utans is in both the public awareness sector and the political sector as well too it is very much an icon".* Soren Mark Jensen, Chief Technical Advisor, Department of Wildlife Sabah, reported in the Daily Express, March 24, 2003.

The rich floodplain and wetlands around Sukau have changed dramatically over the years as the people have moved from traditional economic activity such as fishing to logging and commercial agriculture. The area has an impressive variety of fish and prawns but there are other riches that have attracted businesses. Forestry became the dominant activity in the Kinabatangan from the 1960s to 1980s as logging of the desirable hardwood species reduced many forests in the area.

Since then, the emphasis has moved to growing oil palms to feed the growing global demand for oils and fats. The favorable soil conditions found in the floodplain have made for almost ideal conditions for growing palms and Malaysia now finds itself one of the world's largest producers of palm oil. More than fifty percent of the world's production of palm oil comes from Malaysia and within the Kinabatangan district, oil palms are found on 98 per cent of the land designated for agriculture. No one can travel down the Kinabatangan River without spotting the docks or boats used by the large palm plantations to get their products to market.

Although local communities see the leasing of land to oil palm plantations as a quick way to generate income, there have been some reports indicating that environmental problems are occurring. Plantations have experienced losses from flooding, some fishermen have reported decreases in their catches and barriers to prevent agricultural damage from elephants have been required.

Increasingly, people are seeing that economic activity must be coordinated with environmental protection so that the people of the Kinabatangan basin can enjoy a higher standard of living without sacrificing the area's natural resources that are so unique.

Entada Rheedii on overhangs beside Menanggul River

Sukau fisherman catching prawns

Fishing at Bilit Lake

Sunrise over the mist-shrouded Kinabatangan River

HRH Prince Henrik, Consort of Denmark, on a morning cruise on the Kinabatangan River (2002)

Tug boat pulling logs through mangrove/nipah forest to Sandakan

Oil palm plantation fringing the road to Sukau (1996)

Barge loaded with logs from a riverine area cleared for palm plantation

Mumiang Village

As one step in this process, the government has established a protected space in the lower Kinabatangan. On January 16, 2002, a corridor along the Kinabatangan River was gazetted under the Land Ordinance as the Kinabatangan Wildlife Sanctuary. This gazettement is the result of many years of effort by the Sabah Wildlife Department, Lands and Surveys Department, and the World Wildlife Fund (WWF).

This corridor is important as a wildlife passageway and to protect the river from erosion and pollutants. Unfortunately it is not complete. There are places where logging operations or palm plantations reach to the river's banks. In an effort to preserve this region, the WWF launched the Partners for Wetlands program in 1998. Their vision is to have a forest corridor that connects coastal mangrove swamps with upland forests, to have a floodplain that supports a thriving and diverse economy, and good environmental protection. More information on this program is found in **"Through community partnerships…Bringing hope in the face of threats"** *(refer Page 20)*.

Against this backdrop of increasing pressures on a limited resource, there is a need for models of sustainable development. One of these models is ecotourism, defined as travel to natural areas that promotes conservation of the natural environment, benefits to the host community and learning opportunities for the visitor. Providing tourists with a chance to experience natural areas like the Kinabatangan can support conservation and local development if it is undertaken according to ecotourism principles.

Ecotourism Principles
- Respect the privacy and culture of local people
- Involve the local community in planning
- Hire local people and buy supplies locally where possible
- Orient travelers on the region being visited
- Use guides trained in interpretation of scientific or natural history
- Limit visitation in sensitive natural areas
- Use low impact recreation techniques
- Ensure that wildlife is not harassed
- Support the work of conservation groups preserving the natural areas on which the experience is based

Since 1991, Borneo Eco Tours saw the interest from travelers for trips to the Kinabatangan; and also recognized that there was an opportunity to build a lodge that could enhance the environment instead of harming it, leave money in the local community instead of transferring it to commercial centers, and to educate travelers as well as entertain. The concept of Sukau Rainforest Lodge as a working ecolodge demonstrating that conservation and economic realities could be balanced was born.

"Absolutely fantastic place, untouched jungles and friendly staff. It was really great to experience more or less wildlife after spending all my life in concrete jungles. Looking forward to coming back" Nastia Belikove, Moscow

In the following chapters we will see how Sukau Rainforest Lodge came to be, the challenges in operating in a remote environment, its success in attracting tourists, and the contribution it makes to the conservation of the Kinabatangan.

Green Agamid lizard

Pied hornbill feeding her young

Stick insect

Rhinoceros hornbills feeding on figs

Lesser adjutant stock

Blue eared kingfisher

Egret

Through community partnerships...
Bringing hope in the face of threats

A farmer knows not to kill the goose that lays the golden eggs. In some areas, like Malaysian Borneo's Kinabatangan River, planners and legislators are still struggling to keep the "golden goose" of ecotourism alive. At least half of Borneo's mammals can be found in the floodplain of the Kinabatangan River. This floodplain supports five distinct habitats, home to 10 primate species, 50 mammal and over 200 bird species. It is a rare place; one where visitors can see the unusual Proboscis monkey, gibbons, or an Asian elephant cow and calf herd munching contentedly along the river's edge.

Tourists having a close encounter with wild elephants

The Kinabatangan has been identified as one of the top ecotourism resources in Malaysia, but its future is uncertain. Without a common vision and an interest in preserving the environment, it is difficult to ensure that ecotourism will fulfil its potential here.

Home to several tourism facilities including the Sukau Rainforest Lodge, the lower Kinabatangan River crosses an area heavily dominated by large oil palm plantations. Commercial logging, once active in the region, has been replaced by oil palm cultivation.

The traditional neighbours of the Kinabatangan, the *Orang Sungai* or 'People of the River,' are linked culturally and economically to the forests and river. They, like the wildlife, feel threatened by the loss of forest resources and by the expansion of tourism by outside interests.

Within the tourism industry, there is little incentive for tour operators to be environmentally sensitive. It is left up to the commitment of individual owners. Economies of scale allow larger operators to offer lower prices while consumers do not always recognise the need to pay a premium for a more environmentally-friendly tour.

As an example, poor regulations mean that there is no limit on the number of boats on the river. This leads to crowded waterways with many of the boats carrying large numbers of people, further diminishing the visitors' experience. As well, historical leases allow forests that are close to ecotourism sites to be cleared for agriculture even though it may have disastrous effects on tourism and the environment. Local officials respond to what they perceive as the most urgent concerns.

In an attempt to preserve the Kinabatangan floodplain, the World Wide Fund for Nature (WWF) is undertaking an ambitious project called Partners for Wetlands. This project already has a common vision for the Kinabatangan to be shared among residents, government, conservation groups, and agricultural and tourism interests. Co-ordinated and funded by WWF Netherlands, Partners for Wetlands is dedicated to getting diverse stakeholders to work together. At this point in the process, they are building a vision that includes a "varied landscape supporting a thriving and diverse economy that offers opportunity and choice to local people and businesses... A landscape in which agriculture and nature conservation are united by their common source of vitality – water." The Partners for Wetlands program becomes very important in building support to put conservation and sustainable tourism initiatives higher on the planning agenda.

As tourism is relatively new to the Kinabatangan, Partners for Wetlands is working with stakeholders and partners to develop a management and investment plan for tourism in the area. It will develop opportunities for diversification and stability in the local economy and assist in the search for investors. As a NGO, they hope to build the bridges needed between dissimilar interests to save the Kinabatangan flood-plain. You can follow the progress of Partners for Wetlands at: *www.partnersforwetlands.org* or email *wetlandp@tm.net.my*.

Reprinted from: EcoTourism Management, Winter 2003, Kalahari Management Inc.

Pigtailed macaque

Proboscis monkey

The great Mengaris tree (Koompassia excelsa) towers above the surrounding forest. It is the tallest tree in Sabah and can grow to over 65 metres

Black and yellow Broadbill

Chapter Two

The History of Sukau Rainforest Lodge

"Anyone who has never made a mistake has never tried anything new."
Albert Einstein

In its construction and in its operation, Sukau Rainforest Lodge has tried many new approaches. While some have been more successful than others, it is the underlying philosophy that has made the Lodge unique. A concern for both the natural environment and the people living along the Kinabatangan River has guided Albert Teo and Borneo Eco Tours in their development of the Lodge.

In the late 1980s he started promoting wildlife tours to Sukau after setting up a tour company in 1985. His experiences in this venture generated an interest in building an ecolodge in the area to provide tours to this remote region that would give visitors abundant chances to observe wildlife and to stay in a lodge that did not harm the natural environment they came to enjoy. Thus the concept of an environmentally friendly lodge was born. Albert said "I felt that a wildlife watching trip without an ecolodge as a base was incomplete." In 1990 he began scouting the area to find a suitable building site. "The best site would be one that bordered the Kinabatangan River near the village of Sukau where wildlife was abundant," he said. His preference was for a site on this side of the river with roadside access as it would make building the Lodge and supplying it much easier.

Confident that a suitable building site would be found soon, Borneo Eco Tours Sdn Bhd was formed. This company would become the tour operator for the Sukau Rainforest Lodge, marketing ecotours around the world while Sukau Rainforest Lodge Sdn Bhd would operate the Lodge.

Sukau Rainforest Lodge - Melapi jetty

After spending the summer of 1993 investigating a number of potential sites along the river, he settled on a building site in September 1993. After negotiation with the landowner on the land use, a lease agreement was drawn up which the landowner signed, sealed and registered with the local district council. A deposit and monthly rental was paid as agreed to in the lease and work was started on architectural drawings.

The plan envisioned a 12-room lodge that would be comfortable without relying on modern conveniences such as air conditioning. Guests would be able to see wildlife on river boats operating from the jetty behind the Lodge. These features would allow for spontaneous contacts between guests and nature.

With this vision taking shape and a site in place, everything appeared to be progressing well. It looked like Sukau Rainforest Lodge was about to become a reality. Unfortunately life often has a way of surprising us.

In less than two months Albert put out the call for a contract to build the Lodge. The contract sum that was remitted by the bidders was RM750,000 (US$197,000) which far exceeded the budget. Attempting to deal with the challenge this presented turned out to be the lesser of his worries. While attempting to work out ways to build the Lodge within his budget, he learned that the land he had leased for an ecolodge had meanwhile also been sublet by the landowner to a timber company. The timber company needed a log transit point where their logs could be stockpiled before being shipped down the river or by land to the sawmill. Visiting the site, Albert saw that the land at the proposed building site had been severely degraded with many of the trees removed, and soils and wildlife disturbed. To add insult to injury, the landowner asked for RM40,000 (US$10,500) to level out the ground to make it suitable for building. He sadly decided that this site was no longer suitable and the project for this location was scrapped. He paid off the architect and engineers and cancelled the lease agreement reluctantly at a cost of some RM10,000 (US$2,600).

Anyone who has met Albert knows he is a man with great enthusiasm for new ventures and someone who is not easily dissuaded from his goals. He started the search anew for another suitable building site. In preparation for the construction he hoped would come soon, Sukau Rainforest Lodge Sdn Bhd was registered on November 16, 1993.

In December 1993, a new site had been found. The location was again very conveniently located along the main trunk road to Sukau, but the owner was reluctant to give up the land. After six months of negotiation, the owner was still unwilling to sign a lease agreement. "In hindsight," Albert said, "I realized that there was opposition to the lease from the landowner's family. Local custom has it that if one member in a family does not approve of the lease, the landowner will not sign the lease agreement."

I'm so glad to stay here. I love here. Please Please Please keep it like now for good. I'll come back some day. Thanks a lot!!
Takako Haruyama, Kyoto, Japan
12th September 1995

A Project Timeline
Significant Dates for Sukau Rainforest Lodge

- ➢ 1990 - The search begins for a suitable building site.
- ➢ October 1991 - Borneo EcoTours formed to operate ecotours.
- ➢ September 1993
    - Building site found and lease signed.
    - Architectural drawing and call for contract.
- ➢ November 1993
    - Found site had been significantly degraded and abandoned.
    - Registered Sukau Rainforest Lodge Sdn Bhd.
- ➢ December 1993 – Found second possible building site and negotiated for lease; relatives did not agree to the terms of lease.
- ➢ July 1994 – Looked for third site. Boatman suggests his father's land was available for sale.
- ➢ September 1994 – Loan signed.
- ➢ December 1994
    - Completed purchase of land.
    - Construction started.
- ➢ May 1995
    - Construction finished.
    - Soft opening.
- ➢ November 1995
    - Lodge officially opened by Minister of Tourism, YB Datuk Bernard Dompok.
- ➢ January 1996 – Lodge experiences record flood levels.
- ➢ January 2001 – Kari boardwalk added.
- ➢ May 2002 - Melapi jetty and restaurant completed.
- ➢ January 2003 – Loan approved for Lodge expansion including new Melapi restaurant, rainforest boardwalk, wildlife viewing decks and covered walkways.

Once again, the chosen parcel of land would not be available, but rather than give up at this point, yet another search for a suitable building site for the Lodge was launched. This time Albert was willing to consider looking at any land even if it was located on the opposite side of the river without water and electricity supply. On one of his trips up the river, the Boatman said he thought his father wanted to sell his land. The land in question was not exactly in the shape that he wanted, but he was desperate enough to consider it. It was located 15 minutes by boat across the river from the road and had no electricity. It was an odd-shaped, logged-over second-ary forest, although at 7.11 acres it was certainly big enough for the Lodge. Construction materials would have to be brought in by boat. Juggling the pros and cons of the site in his mind, and looking again at the concept drawings, he reconsidered. Despite the numerous drawbacks of the location, this piece of land did seem to be available. The other hindrances could be dealt with, so Albert decided to buy the land. The most important thing was that this land was for sale, thus offering long term security for the project.

Negotiations started for the land sale. Against local tradition, Kari, the landowner wanted to sell the land, but wanted some assurances that his family would also benefit from the land sale. He requested that Borneo Eco Tours (BET) give precedence where possible to hiring his family members to work at the Lodge. "I sold the land after we discussed the benefit from selling of the land. I decided that is best to sell off the land with the conditions that my children and grandchildren are given the opportunity to work in the Lodge and that when a boat charter is required, our boats will be given priority before the others," Kari said. This proved to be a very wise move on the part of the landowner and also happened to fit in with Albert's concept for the Lodge. While not all the local people have possessed the skills needed at the Lodge, many of the boatman's family have been hired and trained since the Lodge opened, providing economic benefits to the village and important community linkages for Borneo Eco Tours.

Kari's land was gazetted as native title which meant it could only be bought or sold to another native. Albert needed the long term security of land ownership for his investment, but could not buy the land himself. Instead, it was agreed that Kari would sell his land to BET's Director and General Manager, Baton Bijamin, who was a native. Baton then entered into an agreement with BET to lease the land and to assign his property rights to the company.

To complete the construction of the Lodge, Sukau Rainforest Lodge Sdn Bhd. obtained a special government loan for RM500,000 (US$131,600). As the original construction estimates exceeded this amount, Albert had to literally go back to the drawing board. In lieu of an architect and engineers, Albert decided to design the Lodge himself with the help of a draftsman. Once the designs were complete, a new contractor was asked to bid.

Initially a 12-room lodge was considered but discarded in favor of a larger facility of 20 rooms on the new site. That size would still provide for an intimate visitor experience, but be more economical to operate although at a higher initial capital outlay. Albert said, "It will require almost the same effort to manage 20 rooms, but with the same manager's salary and staff wages." The result was that the bid came in well within the project budget at RM350,000 (US$92,100) even with additional rooms.

In December 1994, the Sale and Purchase agreement was completed and the land transfer was registered at the local district council. Construction started almost immediately. Careful planning had been done to work with the physical characteristics of the site. The Lodge was built on stilts to cope with flooding and keep out insects, snakes and other animals and promote air circulation. The buildings were also situated back from the river's edge to allow a corridor for wildlife movement and to maintain the river's natural appearance. It was also important to remove as few trees and vegetation as possible so as to maintain the rainforest setting visitors would expect.

At the time Sukau Rainforest Lodge was being built, the concept of an ecolodge was new and most construction companies were not familiar with practices needed to build such a structure. "After I drew up the Lodge plans and provided them to the construction company, I thought everything was ready to go," Albert said that did not turn out to be the case. When Albert came to inspect the site a week after construction had started, he was horrified to find that the building's footings were encroaching on the neighbor's land and that part of his land had been cleared even though surveyed plans were provided and meetings were held.

The newly completed Lodge (1995)

Sukau Rainforest Lodge (1998)

A typical room at the Lodge (1995)

Official Opening by YB Datuk Bernard Dompok, Minister of Tourism, Culture & Environment (1995)

The mistake had to be corrected and construction of a new foundation and footings, this time in the proper location, had to begin anew. As Albert later said, "It would have been catastrophic if I had come in much later. If I am to do it again, I will definitely pay greater attention to this initial construction stage, stay onsite if necessary to ensure minimal damage to the surrounding vegetation, workmanship is professionally done, piping is properly done."

After that rocky start, construction moved ahead quickly and the Lodge was ready in May 1995 when the first guests arrived. The money challenges were not over. The Landowner approached Albert, saying he wanted an additional payment of RM10,000 (US$2,600) for the land. The landowner had faced many criticisms from the villagers for selling the land to an "outsider". To settle the matter and keep peace with him and the villagers, Albert paid the additional fee.

In November of that year, the Minister of Tourism, YB Datuk Bernard Dompok arrived to officially open the Lodge.

Malaysia Deputy Minister of Culture, Arts & Tourism, YB Dato Teng Gaik Kwan visiting the Lodge

This place is amazing. Luxury away from home! Who would expect such good facilities – hot shower, fan, nice beds and big mirrors, excellent good food in the middle of the jungle? As a government officer, it is good to see a tour operator pursuing the dream advocated by the government. Sukau Rainforest Lodge is definitely a model for ecotourism in Sabah and Malaysia. Keep it up!
Doria Heng, District Surveyor, Land and Survey, Sabah, Malaysia
28th November 1995

In January 1996, Mother Nature celebrated the Lodge opening in her own style by putting the newly-constructed lodge to a test. Flood waters climbed to the highest levels ever recorded for the Kinabatangan River, 15 feet above normal. The water reached the floor level of the newly constructed Lodge creating much concern for everyone; but the foundation held and, fortunately, the waters did not enter the building. The generator was moved out of the room and put on the floating jetty. But guests were able to arrive by boat over flooded ground all the way to the front door steps. They even feasted on river prawns caught with net in what was once the front garden. Everyone knew the Lodge would be able to withstand any natural disaster thrown at it. Plans to entertain and educate visitors were moved forward.

Mother of all floods(1996)

Tourists arriving by boat at what used to be a garden lawn

Recent Developments

With the Lodge enjoying increased popularity and with guests' feedback, a decision to expand the facilities was made in January 2001. First, the Kari boardwalk (named after the first landowner) was completed, allowing guests to move more easily from the Lodge to the river's edge. Then the Melapi jetty was built. Completed in May 2002, this was an important addition to the Lodge as it also served as a restaurant. The Melapi restaurant is popular with visitors, allowing them to dine over the river, catching all the morning's activities while enjoying breakfast and adding a romantic touch to evening meals.

Rainforest Garden

In January 2003, additional bank financing was approved to expand the Lodge facilities which include the new Melapi restaurant cum jetty, a 1,500 foot rainforest boardwalk combining covered walkways with open decks for viewing wildlife. These were completed in late 2003. In 2006, work is expected to start on the construction of three new chalets. These chalets will provide more privacy and room in the rainforest for those people wanting to stay longer or seeking more luxurious accommodation.

Paradise Recipe

Choose a nice part of the Sabah Rainforest,
Place yourself at Sukau Rainforest Lodge,
Together with the one you love,
Add 10KM of the magnificent "Menannggul River"
Mix it with the rich wildlife in the breathtaking surroundings guided by "Mirwan"!
Enjoy the gourmet cooking and Lodge management of "Joseph the Great"!
Blend it all gently,
Garnish on top with "The genuine Malaysian Hospitality",
The composition will result in a Good slice of Paradise!

Thank you.

Seriye Ganslandt & Rutget Ganslandt/ Sweden
3rd – 5th March 2002

Melapi Restaurant cum jetty (2002)

The new recreation deck (2004)

Kari Boardwalk (2002)

Harmonizing ambience at the Boardwalk

Black-naped Blue Monarch

Strategic Planning

Initially the Sukau Rainforest Lodge project faced a daunting set of challenges. Building an ecolodge is a significant undertaking and can entail considerable business risk. Great financial investment is required to build a lodge of sufficient size to be economically viable. Adhering to ecotourism principles during construction and operation often requires you to seek out new technologies and operate without product warranties. In all, attempting to meet a triple bottom line of social, economic and environmental goals challenges even the most seasoned tourism professional .

> If this was all we did in Borneo, it was worth coming all this way for the boat trip alone. Keep the area just as it is. Do not over commercialize it or you'll lose it all for good and it is too precious to do that.
> *Graham Hallihan, Victoria, Australia*
> 8th July 1995
>
> Two wonderful days at Sukau Rainforest Lodge. Varano, some alive and one dead, snakes, Proboscis monkeys, macaques, eagles, bearded pigs, hornbills, elephants puh, leeches on Fernando, butterflies, egrets, kingfisher and a most majestic Orangutan male, you name it, we've seen it all. On top of all that we got excellent food, cold beer and wine plus awesome service in a most relaxing environment. VIVA ECOTOURISM!!
> *Revisor Group, Sweden*
> 18th November 1999

When Albert decided he wanted to construct an ecolodge, he undertook a planning exercise known as a Strength Weakness Opportunities Threat or SWOT analysis. This planning technique allows an organization such as Borneo Eco Tours to examine a situation and decide whether it should proceed with a business opportunity. It can also provide insight into how a project will need to be marketed or managed in order to survive.

The SWOT analysis on Sukau Rainforest Lodge revealed many strengths, indicating the project would likely succeed, but also some areas of weaknesses and threats that would require careful planning to avoid disaster. The results of this analysis are described in the following sections.

Strengths

1. The area has great wildlife. It is one of two known sites in the world with ten species of primates in one location. In addition, four of the species are found only in Borneo.

2. It is very easy to spot and view wild Proboscis monkey in the area. This is as a result of the monkey's need to find safe roosting spots along the river each evening. The Proboscis will seek out the high branches in the large trees that line the Kinabatangan River and sit with their backs to the water. In the event that a predator approaches, the monkeys will be alerted in time to jump into the river and escape. So tourists can easily spot the monkeys in the late evening and early mornings along the river banks.

3.   Bird watching conditions are optimum along the Kinabatangan. The river's wide breadth makes it easy to spot birds and there are plenty of them. More than 265 species of birds, including all eight species of hornbill are found here. In addition, bird watchers can see the rare Storm stork and the Oriental darters.

4.   It is easy to spot Borneo's Pygmy elephants as they migrate past the Lodge and along the river banks. The Pygmy elephant has just recently been recognized as a distinct species. It differs from the Asian elephant by its smaller stature and less aggressive demeanor. Given the small population of this species, the opportunity to view these animals will be highly sought after by wildlife watchers.

> Experiencing the wonders of nature in this eco-system is a memorable experience. The treasures here are beyond the price of jewels. Preserve the habitat!
> *Rosemary Holt, Pennsylvania, USA*
> 29th May 1995
>
> I had the most fun watching the Proboscis monkeys. They put on a great show with their tree leaping, talking and one even did a belly flop in the water while attempting to jump across the river. And now, I know the true color of a hornbill.
> *Tosca/Canada*
> 1st June 1995

5.   The boat ride from Sandakan to Sukau is very scenic and allows for viewing of many unique vegetation types in addition to occasional sightings of Orang-utans and elephant.

6.   The land near the Lodge has received environmental protection. In 2000, 26,000 hectares of land along the Kinabatangan River was gazetted into the Kinabatangan Wildlife Sanctuary. In addition, WWF Malaysia has spearheaded the Partners For Wetland project to generate additional support for conservation practices in the region.

> Fabulous! The staff, the food, the atmosphere and the company of other guests have all contributed to make this a memorable holiday. The birds and animals magnificent topped off by sighting a herd of elephants.
> *John and Mary Gatley, Australia*
> 6th – 8th May, 2002

Weaknesses

1.   The Sukau area is subject to annual flooding. As commercial agriculture, logging and other activities place additional pressure on the environment it is possible greater flooding could occur.

2.   It is difficult to find trained staff in the local area. For those people hired from the local area, it can be hard to develop a work culture that meets the needs of the hospitality industry.

3.   The area surrounding Sukau has been logged in the past so that vegetation seen is secondary forest. This includes the newly gazetted Lower Kinabatangan Wildlife Sanctuary. Many visitors will not be aware of this fact or be bothered by it, but for others, it may make a visit to Danum Valley and its virgin rainforest a more attractive option.

4.   The roads into Sukau are poor. The last 43 kilometers are on gravel road making for a rough trip. Vehicle maintenance costs are high.

5. Transferring visitors to Sukau by road does not give them a good experience. In addition to the rough roads, the view is disturbing. For most of the 120 kilometers, the view is of palm oil plantations stretching from one horizon to another.

6. There is a limited supply of local foodstuffs for purchase. Most food items and supplies must be delivered from Sandakan to Sukau, a distance of 130 kilometers overland or 2 hours by boat. Purchasing locally is more desirable from an ecotourism perspective and less expensive, but supply is limited.

Threats

"Only after the last tree has been cut down, only after the last river has been poisoned, only after the last fish has been caught, only then will you find that money cannot be eaten." An old Cree Indian saying

1. As Sukau has become a popular destination for nature lovers, more and bigger boats have been touring the area's rivers and streams. If no controls are put on the number and type of boats, overcrowding of the waterways could occur. The noise, pollution and disturbance of Proboscis monkey habitat could harm the environment and the visitor's experience.

2. If the number of tourists increases without the local community receiving economic benefits, the support shown to tourism activities by residents could diminish.

3. As more staff are successful in securing and retaining employment at the Lodge, their increasing affluence could upset the harmony of the community and create jealousy among neighboring villages.

4. Commercial agriculture is a vital part of the Sabah economy. As land is converted to commercial palm oil plantations, it poses a threat to ecotourism as scenic views are altered and habitat is decreased. For species like elephants, these developments are particularly troublesome; when they wander into private lands the number of human-animal conflicts increase. Often the elephants are the losers and wildlife viewing opportunities for tourists decrease.

5. With five other lodges in the Sukau area, there is stiff price competition. This competition can discourage lodge owners from upgrading their products or result in cost cutting at the expense of wildlife and the environment. Sukau Rainforest Lodge would need to convince travelers that the Lodge's ecotourism philosophy merits a price premium.

A brilliant blend of ecology and comfort. The food was excellent, the guides knowledgeable, and the whole effort was done with a thought to the environment.
Scott Schoenfeld, USA
15th-17th January 2002

We are family with two girls in the age of 8 and 10 years old. We all think it is a wonderful place. We wish you all the best for the fortune.
Ronny Jansson & family, Sweden
25th January 2002

Opportunities

1. The Lower Kinabatangan floodplain and the Lodge's proximity to it provide unique accommodation and tour opportunities to experience Borneo's riverine rainforest.

2. The successful establishment of an ecolodge will provide alternative employment choices for people who do not want to work in palm plantations.

3. The creation of an ecolodge will allow Borneo Eco Tours to diversify the ecotourism products they offer in Sabah. It will also provide partnership opportunities with other tour operators who are looking for a sustainable tourism product.

4. By providing a wildlife safari experience, Sukau Rainforest Lodge can provide a world-class trip that will appeal to international tourists looking for unique wildlife-watching destinations.

> We loved this place, the wildlife, the nature and the food. The people are so nice and our guide was excellent. Thanks for everything and we are back in a few years!
> Patricia Frei, Switzerland
> 8th May 2002

When Albert and his team of managers reviewed the results of the SWOT analysis they felt they could manage the possible threats and weaknesses while capitalizing on their strengths and the potential market opportunities. It was a risk that seemed worthwhile taking and had the strategic potential to distinguish Borneo Eco Tours from other tour operators. Almost a decade and many awards later, we can see that the risk has paid off. In the next chapters we will delve into how the Lodge has come to be an internationally recognized example of sustainable tourism practices.

> I hope this centre in the forest is the Model for the next millennium.
> *Jeremy Lovd, Switzerland*
> 9th October 1998
>
> This place is really something to be proud of. We have had some of our best days here. Excellent cruises, good food and staff that look after you the very best way.
> *Per Claesson, Sweden, ABC Tours*
> 31st January 2000
>
> So wild, so beautiful. Keep this place for ever.
> *Daniel and Daniele, Reunion Island, France*
> 11th March 2000
>
> Simply Superb! A fabulous experience. Truly a day of National Geographic! The guides were excellent and the hospitality outstanding. We will return with very favourable memories of Sukau and Borneo. We will certainly return. Thanks for everything.
> *Sandra Lindsey, President, Asian Journeys, California, USA*
> 22nd October 1995

Melapi Restaurant overlooking the Kinabatangan River (2002)

Dinner by candlelight

Garnet Pitta

Chapter Four

Building an Ecolodge

"The most rewarding things you do in life are often the ones that look like they cannot be done." Arnold Palmer

What exactly is an ecolodge? Many people are somewhat confused by the term and do not understand how it is any different from other small hotels or lodges. But an ecolodge does have unique characteristics taking environment impact principles into the very design and construction. The design of an ecolodge will take advantage of the local environment; for example, positioning windows to use prevailing winds for cooling instead of air conditioners. An ecolodge will minimize the impact of the actual building footprint and have an architecture style that matches the environment and local culture. Energy reduction and resource conservation will be evident throughout an ecolodge in the choice of fuel sources, shower heads, toilets, waste disposal methods, or composting of kitchen wastes. Wherever possible, local materials will be used for construction and often, local people will be involved in the building or furnishing of the lodge.

At Sukau Rainforest Lodge we can see evidence of these unique ecolodge features. The guests of Borneo Eco Tours had been staying in tourist lodges for some years but none had the style Albert envisioned. "Since we were a tour operator specializing in ecotourism, we had to have a good ecolodge with the same consistent philosophy and high standards to complement our tours," he said.

As we learned in Chapter Two, there are challenges in making this vision a reality. It took a couple of attempts to come up with design plans that were within budget and finding a site for the ecolodge was a major challenge. The ideal place must have abundant wildlife and infrastructure in the form of transportation links and power. The final site met some of his requirements, but had only boat access and with no connection to the power grid. This location added to the challenges inherent in building an ecolodge such as the Sukau Rainforest Lodge.

Everything had to be moved to Sukau by barge from Sandakan. This would mean shipping large quantities of sand, gravel, cement, steel bars, and lumber. Only water, mud and bugs were readily available at the building site. For the initial construction phase, the contractor ventured to Sandakan for supplies. But to build a lodge that was comfortable and functional, local materials should be used wherever possible. This would adhere to ecotourism principles and provide visitors with an ambience that is unique to Malaysian Borneo. After much consideration it was decided that the timber for the Lodge would come from Borneo hardwood species such as Belian, Merbau, Nyatoh, and Selangan Batu. Tropical cane would be used for finishing and for those areas needing more ventilation.

Once all the building materials were located, arrangements were made to get them to the Lodge site. As the road only reaches the village of Sukau and the last part of the road is pitted with very large potholes, travel overland is laborious. The contractor decided it would be more economical to move everything by water from Sandakan and a barge was hired.

With his designs in hand and supplies arriving any day, Albert moved ahead with construction. The contractor hired was very experienced in the building industry but had not built an ecolodge before. He knew how to construct traditional structures, but was not familiar with ecotourism principles. And, although he had been given sufficient information on the unique features of an ecolodge, problems did arise. The main one occurred when the contractor overlooked the need to keep the building site as natural as possible throughout construction. In the first week, Albert was horrified to notice that the Lodge footprint was encroaching on neighbouring land and several trees had been cut down. One large tree that was spared was the giant "Belunu" fruit tree (*Mangifera Caesia Jack*). The locals believe this is where the spirits would dwell and would bring bad luck if anyone were to disturb it. Fortunately, the problem was discovered early in the construction process and the footings could still be moved; the vegetation would eventually recover. One of the trees, Bongkol Kuning *(Nauclea Subdita)*, is today (nine years later) twenty feet high. He and his contractor worked more closely after this to ensure that ecotourism practices were observed.

Work progressed slowly during the construction phase as it coincided with the rainy season. A rainforest is a complex ecosystem with the plants forming a protective layer over the soil. With the vegetation removed for the actual building site, the soil rapidly turned to a muddy mess. "It was like a minefield in the depth of the Borneo rainforest with yellow coloured potholes emerging everywhere as the footings were dug," Albert remembers with a grimace. No workers were hurt during the construction, but they were covered in mud much of the time and it got worse as the rainy season progressed. "So much mess and construction materials. It was depressing in the beginning to see this destruction, but with the passing months, things began to look better as the building took shape and the vegetation quickly recovered," Albert said.

Artist Impressions

In the early stages of construction, the site looked scarred from the construction, but the Lodge footprint was relatively small as every effort had been made in the design phase to use land wisely. Additions would be made later, but the initial Lodge had four blocks of rooms, a large building with the restaurant, kitchen, gift shop and lounge, and open sundeck. These buildings were linked together around a landscaped garden and placed on stilts to improve circulation and reduce the chance of snakes or other wildlife mingling with the guests in their rooms.

SRL Chalet A

SRL Chalet B

All of the planning paid off. When the Lodge was finished in May 1995, it would become clear that most of the building site was undisturbed. Only 12,000 square feet out of a land area of 310,000 square feet or four per cent was used for construction.

SRL Chalet C

Finding local workers to build the Lodge proved to be another challenge. The plan was to create jobs in the community as had been promised to Kari, the original landowner. The contractor was asked to hire men from the local community. Local people were found and put on the payroll, but this move did not turn out as well as hoped.

The men did not have experience nor work culture in building structures as specialized as the Lodge. In the end, the contractor had to bring in work crews from Sandakan and other parts of Sabah to complete the Lodge.

Relations with the community were strained during the construction phase and the early days of the Lodge's operation. The purchase of the site from Kari was a departure from long held traditions and some people were uneasy with the changes. For many months, local people, especially relatives of the land owner, made visits to the Lodge to complain about their concerns with the break in tradition. "We faced many challenges from the local people," Baton Bijamin, General Manager and Director for Borneo Eco Tours and Sukau Rainforest Lodge recounted, "They came to the Lodge nearly everyday threatening the manager and staff." This discontent would continue into the early days of the Lodge's operation, but Albert made continuous efforts to be a good neighbour and to justify Kari's faith in him.

Baton Bijamin

With the completion of the main contract, it was time to ship in the solar collector equipment, generator, and furniture and fixtures. Most of these items would need to come from Kota Kinabalu, some 350 kilometres away. With soft furnishings coming from different suppliers and factories, it was difficult to coordinate a single barge trip. Instead it was decided that everything would be transported overland. This would mean a ten hour lorry trip to Sukau village.

Once at the village, SRL chartered boats to bring everything from towels and bed sheets to tables and chairs across the river to the Lodge. "All the staff would then lend a hand to carry them to the Lodge from the jetty," Albert said. This proved to be a very time consuming task as a mountain of kitchen equipment, bedroom fixtures and fittings, mattresses, and curtains had to be moved one item at a time. Albert turned to a dedicated work crew: "My General Manager, Baton Bijamin, and I brought our whole families there in the last week. Everyone chipped in to fit the curtain rails, shower rails, and hang window and shower curtains, and hangers".

In addition to the unique steps taken during construction, the Lodge needed to install technology to minimize resource consumption during daily operations. In the following sections we will look closer at the technology that was needed to put the "eco" into the Lodge.

Water Systems

One resource theLodge had in abundance was rain and river water. There would be challenges in collecting it, but the Lodge's location in a rainforest would mean frequent periods of heavy rainfall would provide a steady source of clean drinking water. A system was set up to collect rainwater from the Lodge's metal roofing which had been chosen for this purpose, and piped it to liner tanks via water collection tanks. Guests will not be at the Lodge very long before they become aware of these large black storage tanks. They are stacked in several places on the grounds and loom over the curious observer. These tanks cost RM450 (US$120) each but hold 400 gallons making them valuable tools in water conservation. The water collected in these tanks is filtered before it is used for cooking and drinking.

Water is also taken from the Kinabatangan River during periods of heavy usage and in the dry season. An electric pump moves the silt laden water to a series of water tanks, treated with aluminium sulphate and left for 24 hours for sediments to settle before being drained to lower level water tanks for another 24 hours. This process is repeated three times. It is then piped by gravity flow to the liner tank. Water is then pumped to a 25 foot gravity tank that is used to supply guest rooms with water for showers and toilets.

Working out the engineering for this water system provided yet another challenge. In addition to figuring out how to gather and use rainwater, piping had to be run to each of the guest rooms and the kitchen. When SRL was ready for its first trial run, it turned out to be a wet experience all around as leaks were found in almost every room. The plumbers were quickly put into action with all the pipes being tightened again, a slow and time consuming process. Finally it was time for another check and this time the piping held! They were ready to go. This was a far cry from the custom of bathing in the river observed by the villagers living along the river.

Does Ecotourism Mean a Lack of Visitor Comfort?

Visitors not familiar with the concept of an ecolodge may fear they will suffer from a lack of creature comforts. Nothing could be further from the truth at Sukau Rainforest Lodge. Visitors can relax knowing that they will be very comfortable while traveling in an environmentally friendly way.

The Lodge was designed to minimize energy conservation but visitors need not be bothered by the high midday temperatures. Guest rooms have large, louvered windows and high ceilings to keep them cool. Instead of air conditioning, ceiling fans are installed in each room to supplement Sukau's natural breezes.

Each guest room has twin beds, a dressing table with mirror, a luggage rack and a attached bathroom with hot shower, wash basin and western-style toilet.

There is ample room to relax at the Lodge with three sets of rattan sofas, a library, magazine rack, and restaurant seating for 40 in the main building. Benches and chairs are found on the open walkways for those wanting to watch birds or monkeys moving through the forest. More tables and chairs are found on the newly-completed Melapi jetty restaurant which allows guests to write in their journals and observe the daily rhythms along the river.

SUKAU RAINFOREST LODGE

Shoplot 12A, 2nd Floor, Lorong Bernam 3, Taman Soon Kiong,
88300 Kota Kinabalu, Sabah, Malaysia
Tel: 60 88 234009   Fax: 60 88 233688
info@borneooecotours.com   www.borneoecotours.com

WATER USAGE GUIDELINES

Activity	Method adopted	Qty. Used Ltr.	Method to be adopted	Qty. required Ltr.	Qty. saved Ltr.
Brushing Teeth	Running tap for 5 min.	45	Tumbler or Glass	0.5	44.5
Washing Hands	Running tap for 2 min	18	Half filled wash basin	2	16
Shaving	Running tap for 2 min.	18	Shaving mug	0.25	17.75
Shower	Letting Shower run while soaping staying under Shower too long	90	Wet down tap off, soap up, rinse off	20	70
Flushing Toilet	Using old fashioned large capacity cistern	13.5 or more	Dual System short flush liquid waste, Full flush solid waste	4.5 9.0	4.5 or more
Watering Plants	Running hose for 5 minutes	120	Water can	5	115
Washing Floor	Running hose for 5 minutes	200	Mop and bucket	18	182
Washing Car	Running hose for 10 minutes	400	Buckets (Two)	18	382

1) Our lodge is 100% self-sufficient in water. To minimise water wastage, our shower head is specially fitted to use only 6.5 litres of water per minute or 32.5 litres / 8.5 US gallons every five minutes.

2) Hot water is supplied by 2 units of 132 gallons of Solarhart 300 JK solar heating systems.

3) The water level in the toilet cistern has been adjusted to minimise water usage.

4) Please help us to conserve water by minimising toilet flushing and by turning off tap and shower when brushing and shampooing.

Educating Guests on Water Usage

Although guests do not have to forgo personal hygiene routines when visiting Sukau, some education is required on water usage. Hot water for bathing is generated by running rainwater through two Solarhart 300 JK solar heating systems. Each unit can heat 132 gallons at a time ensuring that water is available during the busy evening times when guests are cleaning up for dinner. Shower heads are specially fitted to only use 6.5 litres of water per minute or 32.5 litres/8.5 US gallons every five minutes. Most visitors to the Lodge will enjoy these showers without much thought to their size or the mechanical design that went into making them work. This was not the case for some of the Lodge's first visitors. Baton Bijamin remembers being very nervous in the Lodge's first days about the power and water systems' abilities to function smoothly. One day as everyone was getting used to the new routines, someone forgot to pump water from the liner tank to the gravity tank. "We only found out when a guest came out from their room with shampoo on their head," said Baton. This does not happen anymore, but is a funny reminder of how many details go into making an ecolodge run smoothly.

Visitors to Sukau will find that even brushing their teeth is educational as friendly reminders are posted in each bathroom suggesting people take short showers and turn off the water off while shampooing in the shower or brushing their teeth. By having information provided to them on how much water is saved by these simple steps, visitors can savour the satisfaction of conserving resources during their daily activities.

> At last, living proof that a country and local community can benefit from tourism without destroying the environment or compromising traditions. Soundless electric motors on locally made boats, solar power, energy conservation, controlled landscaping, employing the local community are all examples worthy of the label of "Ecotourism". Bravo. Bagus-lah! Keep up the good work and I'll spread the word.
> *Vijay Tohani, Belfast, Northern Ireland*
> 8th July 1995

In keeping with the Lodge's environmental philosophy, toilet cistern levels have been adjusted to minimize water usage and guests are asked to flush less.

Waste Disposal

Disposal of effluents is always a concern in remote locations; without proper treatment sewage and other wastes can contaminate rivers and ground water. Sukau Rainforest Lodge is equipped with proper septic tanks so nothing is discharged into the river. Organic materials like food scraps from the kitchen are composted. Non-biodegradable materials are separated and sent to Sukau or Sandakan for disposal and recycling.

Guests are encouraged to deposit recyclable items such as aluminium cans and plastic or glass bottles on site in bins labelled "cans", "bottles" and "plastics". These are found on the open deck near the Lodge.

Getting staff used to proper disposal of waste instead of the river took time. In many parts of Asia, people living close to the ocean or rivers have traditionally disposed of everything by dumping it in the water. Albert wanted to change these habits, but knew it would take time to change long-ingrained patterns. Through repeated reminders and explanations on how important recycling or proper waste disposal was for the environment, people started to catch on and much less went into the river.

Electricity and Lighting

The location of the Sukau Rainforest Lodge site, across the river from the village, would require it to find it's own power sources. The initial plans were to provide sufficient electricity to run lights, fridges and other equipment from a solar power system. Twenty Siemens solar photo-vol-taic panels were installed on the Lodge's roof. They are connected to 4 GNB long-life dry-cell batteries and a 3 KW Trace Pure Sinewave power inverter to provide a steady source of power. In one of those unexpected twists of nature, the cloudy periods that accompany the frequent rains and the mists that sometime hang over the region make it difficult to generate sufficient power from the solar panels alone. During the daytime, only 30% of the Lodge's power needs could come from the solar panels.

Solar water heater, with water tank in the background

A 15 KVA generator was added to the Lodge to supplement the solar system so that there was a 24 hour a day consistent supply of power. This was later augmented with a 25KVA generator as dry-cell batteries could no longer hold the charge after six years usage and were reluctantly phased out. Guests are encouraged to turn off their lights and ceiling fans when they are not in their room to help reduce the amount of power the Lodge must produce. Regular 40-watt light bulbs at the Lodge have been replaced with special 9-watt fluorescent bulbs to further reduce energy use.

Recycled cooking oil lamp

Lighting in the evening is supplemented by kerosene oil lamps in the garden and along the corridors. Recycled cooking oil is used in the lamps found in the restaurant and lounge area, providing guests with an exotic, cosy ambience while eliminating the need to dispose of the oil.

> It was a very nice day and a very romantic evening, in very strong rain and a candlelight dinner. We love this place. Thank you.
> *Birgit Miller, Cologne, Germany*
> 13th September 1995

Noise

Anyone staying at the Lodge quickly comes to appreciate the sounds of the rainforest. The call of a hornbill, the crashing of branches as Proboscis monkeys leap from tree to tree, or the steady hum from the cicadas are common sounds. At night, the sounds are different, but no less interesting. Albert wanted to ensure that guests had the chance to experience these forest sounds instead of listening to the drone of an air conditioner. To ensure this happened, the Lodge was designed on an open concept. Rooms have screened windows with ceiling fans for cooling. Guests are encouraged to observe quiet time in their rooms after 9:00 p.m. while the less inclined can stay up and socialise at the lounge area. This early quiet time may be a bit different for guests not used to being told to observe quiet time, but as most people are pleasantly tired from their day's adventures, guests look forward to turning in early with a rainforest symphony to lull them to sleep!

The generator at the Lodge has noise reduction acoustic insulation to keep noise levels down during the day. It is also used to charge the dry-cell batteries for the electric motors used on the river cruise.

Being a skilled photographer and observer of wildlife, Albert knew from personal experience that allowing his guests to move quietly through the forest would greatly increase their chances of seeing animals. Much of the wildlife watching in the Sukau area occurs from the waterways. People in boats can approach animals easily and quietly with small electric motors. While the boats may use larger gas motors to cover longer distances, SRL was the

Electric-powered motor

first lodge to identify the environmental and aesthetic benefits of using electric motors when the boats were approaching wildlife. Interestingly, he got the idea from a friend in Tampa, Florida who used a similar motor for fishing. Indeed the intimate nature of these boat cruises as visitors silently view and photograph the abundant flora and fauna of the Kinabatangan, without the need to worry about vibration and smelling the oil fumes, are the main focus for most tourists. As Albert told one Lodge visitor: "You will love the riverboat cruise. Some people say it is the highlight of their lives, the best time they have had."

Black and Red Broadbills

Estuarine Crocodile

Quiet cruising on electric-powered motor boat

Hire Locally, Buy Locally

Hire locally, buy locally is a critical ecotourism principle and the Lodge has demonstrated creativity in adapting this principle to its operation. A concerted effort to hire local people to help build the Lodge and local craftsmen were brought to the Lodge to bring out the elements of traditional architecture. Some of the furniture was made locally and crafts created by local women are featured in the gift shop. Initially, proceeds from the gift shop went to non-governmental agencies such as WWF Malaysia and Sabah Society For The Blind. In 1999, this practice was replaced when the Sukau Ecotourism Research and Development Centre (SERDC) was created. Now SERDC collects US$1 for every guest who stays at the Lodge. This money goes towards research and community and environmental projects.

SRL encourages people to start their own businesses with the Lodge as a major customer. Awang, the son-in-law of Kari, the original landowner, was encouraged to start a boat-building business to supply boats to the Lodge. He and another neighbour, Ghani, did this and crafted the boats that are so popular with many of the Lodge visitors. These boats are built in the traditional local Orang Sungai style and hold only eight guests at a time. With a maximum of eight guests, often less, visitors enjoy their own window seat and a much more intimate experience than found with the boats of competing lodges where often 25 people are crowded into a larger and much noisier boat. SRL boats have the four-stroke outboard engines needed to cover long distances quickly, but are unique from the other lodges in that each boat also has a small electric motor that becomes the main locomotion when approaching and photographing wildlife and when travelling the small waterways.

> Best of all lodges/camps we have stayed in. Excellent food, friendly and efficient service, wonderful environment. Very relaxing. Drifting silently up the Menunggul River hearing and seeing the wildlife great experience. Well done on all your Green initiatives. Up the Creek without a paddle, but a silent motor. Superlatives abound – thanks for a wonderful time and for teaching me to play Malaysian poker and Kerang.
> *John, Robert and James Macfarlane, Halam, England*   24th July 1996
>
> Well set out, plenty of food. The electric motors are fabulous for the river cruise. Keep the size of boats they are. The larger boats we saw on the river looked very out of place.
> *Phil Youdale, Borneo Tours Specialist, Sydney, Australia*   9th July 1998

Food at the Lodge is based around local dishes such as sweet and sour fish, chicken kurma, beef redang, and mixed stir-fried vegetables. When available, fish and river prawns are purchased from local fishermen where they have more than they need for personal consumption. One of the local cooks was sent to train at a restaurant in Sandakan while the rest are now well trained by Joseph Chong, the Lodge manager, and visitors can now be assured of excellent food during their stay at Sukau.

Lodge Employees Recall
The Excitement of Working in The Jungle

One day while doing some work at the Lodge one of the staff came running and told me that there was a herd of elephants passing just behind our Lodge in the forest. Excited because it was the first time we had elephants passing so close, we hurriedly went to the trail to take a closer look at the animals. We decided that those of us who had never seen an elephant at close range should go first. The group was made up of the cook and his assistant, two of the housekeeping girls, a replacement student Therese, the Lodge supervisor Elmo, Jaini, and me.

Awang building the jetty for SRL

Awang with his boats ordered by Borneo Eco Tours

Amad with his new prized outboard engine in exchange for contract work at the Lodge

Albert (left), Joseph and Adrian (right) with a group of American tourists

We decided the best and safest way to approach the elephants would be by walking along the trail that already existed behind the Lodge. We saw many new trails created by the elephants, but we didn't see a single elephant even though we could hear them trumpet call now and then. Without knowing it at the time we were heading straight into the middle of the herd as we walked further along the trail. There was no sign of elephant until we were about two thirds of the way down the trail. Then we saw the first elephant. On the left side of the trail there was a baby elephant with its back turned to us, munching contentedly on young rattan shoots. We thought we were very lucky to have such a good look at the elephant without it noticing us, until it turned and came face-to-face with our group. The moment it saw us, the elephant charged and we had no choice, but to run for our lives. I was lucky to avoid being rammed by the elephant when I instinctively jumped to one side as it passed only inches from me. Our troubles were not over yet, as at that instant the mother decided to chase us. We managed to outrun her when she got stuck chasing us through some dense bush. We counted ourselves lucky as we realized that if she had not been stopped by the vegetation she could have easily overtaken us. We knew now that we had inadvertently gotten between the baby and his mother and that the first charge and the subsequent chase were only a reaction to the perceived threat our presence made. In the excitement of escaping from the elephants we did not realize that Elmo had got caught in the liana (a sturdy tropical vine) when he was running out of the forest. It was strange how during that critical moment a man can gain superhuman strength and easily break through a liana to escape from danger. Elmo literally tore the liana in two to escape from certain death. When we returned later to see the liana, it was bigger than a man's wrist and we could not tear it in two like Elmo had, no matter how hard we tried!

When our group had reached a safe place away from the mother elephant, everyone decided they had had enough wildlife watching and decided to return to the Lodge. I realized however, that I had not taken any pictures of the elephants even though I had a camera around my neck the whole time. I decided to try for a picture of the elephants. I told the group to go ahead while I stayed back to take some pictures. Just as they disappeared from sight, I heard the trumpet calls from a herd of elephants nearby. Panic-stricken, I tried to run down the path the other people had taken, but it was now blocked by elephants. The elephants were coming from all directions. Fortunately, they had not noticed me yet, but I thought it was only a matter of time because there was no way to escape. Then I saw a tall tree in front of me. Without a second thought, I just ran, jumped onto the tree, and climbed until I reached a height of about thirty feet above the ground.

From my perch in the tree I kept still and watched the scene below me. There must have been at least forty elephants. Some of them were using their trunks to smell the ground, and were kicking at the dirt where my group had been hidden only a few minutes earlier. I told myself that if the group had stayed there, the elephants would have discovered them in no time at all. After a few minutes, the elephants turned their attention from the ground to the sky.

They started to lift their trunks and smell the air above them. I thought, "Wow, if they know I'm here, they will definitely pull down this tree I'm in." I remembered, with fright, the story told by the villagers who had explained that when a group of elephants had wanted to pull down a coconut tree, the whole herd would pee around the tree until the ground was softened, then push and pull the tree using their heads and trunks until it fell over. I did not want this to happen to the tree I was in, so I kept very quiet, praying that they would not notice me, and that they would leave soon. The few minutes I waited, unobserved, in the tree felt like ages, but I was glad that I was able to observe the elephants and I actually remembered to take a few photos.

Half an hour later, the elephants moved back into the forest and I took the opportunity to climb down the tree. I ran quickly back to the Lodge with my camera still dangling around my neck. Arriving back there, I told the staff of my adventure and we all enjoyed a good laugh. Inside my heart, I promised myself that I would never do that sort of stunt anymore.

Adrian Migiu
Lodge Manager 1996 to 2000

[This story shows that working near elephants can have its exciting moments as another Lodge employee, Jaini Amad, found out in his recollections below.]

I was with John handling a film crew from the USA that was hosted by Jeff Corwin. We were on an assignment to track a herd of elephants from a nearby forest in Sukau. Not until we were in the middle of the forest did we realize that we were also in the middle of the herd that we were searching for. The elephants had been resting for awhile, but they suddenly awoke as they realized we were there. The elephants starting trumpeting and raising their trunks in the air. It was chaotic! I became so panicked that I was struck dumb. When the elephants realized we meant them no harm and the situation calmed down, one of the film crew asked me why my pants were wet when it was not raining. I told him I was sweating. That was not quite the truth, but I was embarrassed and started to make my way back to the Lodge before them. They all laughed at me during the incident, but fortunately that was the worst that happened that day.

Jaini Amad,
Lodge Supervisor

Rhinoceros Hornbill

Financing

If you are looking for peace, tranquility and wildlife, look no more – this is it! The concept of this nature reserve (lodge) is commendable and should be supported. The staff is friendly and knowledgeable. We've been here three days and enjoyed every moment.
Ben and Maria Lee, USA
2nd November 2003

Finding the money to start an ecolodge is extremely problematic for most entre-preneurs. Banks in general are reluctant to finance tourism businesses, and regard ecotourism with a cautiousness reserved for their riskiest investments. Sukau Rainforest Lodge was successful in securing financing because Albert Teo had an established tourism business, Borneo Eco Tours, and many years of related industry experience. The expertise he gained from managing the Shangri-La Hotel in Kota Kinabalu, and his years in running a tour company had given him the management background so important to creditors and investors.

When Albert finally found the right site for Sukau Rainforest Lodge, he knew it was time to secure a bank loan for the project. Even with his proven track record, most banks were reluctant to lend money for the Lodge because of its remote location. The distance from major cities and its unique character would make it difficult for a bank to recoup its investment defaulted on the loan.

After meeting with numerous bankers, SRL was able to find one that would take a chance on the project. The banker considered the risk level acceptable but only if the company directors would provide additional guarantees. Each director was asked to provide personal guarantees for the loan and collateral in addition to the Lodge itself. This was a hardship for the directors in the early days, but fortunately their instincts on the project's potential were correct and the guarantees were not called upon.

The interest rate on this first loan was 6.5%, competitive with other loans, but the term was only five years. This proved to be too short for the Lodge to generate sufficient cash flow to cover both operating expenses and loan repayments, so investors had to inject additional funds to replenish working capital. He was lucky to find some local people who were interested in the project and convinced them to become shareholders in Sukau Rainforest Lodge. Through their investments these silent shareholders now own 30 per cent of the company while Albert holds the remaining 70 per cent.

Over those first five years, shareholders had to contribute an additional RM450,000 (US$ 118,000) to repay the loan and increase the working capital. In effect, they contributed almost as much as the original loan. In addition to these contributions, the directors helped build up working capital by not drawing any salary for the first three years. As well during periods of low business, its associate company, Borneo Eco Tours, helped to cover negative cash flows. Even today they receive only a nominal sum. Clearly ecotourism requires investors to measure success in non-ma-terial terms!

Sukau Rainforest Lodge Financing Sources			
Item	Time Period	Amount (RM)	Use
Loan	1994	500,000	Lodge construction
Shareholders contribution	1993 - 1997	450,000	Repayment of loan, increase working capital
Loan	2003	550,000	Lodge expansion

In 2003, when plans were developed to expand the Lodge to provide more visitor amenities, further bank financing was needed. The Asian financial crisis and a recession in Malaysia had created a need for government action to stimulate the Malaysian economy. The government responded by creating a stimulus package for the tourism industry which included loan incentives. Albert saw this as an opportunity to get more financing at an affordable rate and quickly submitted an application. Given the Lodge's ability to meet its earlier repayment schedule, it was deemed to be a worthy credit risk and a RM 550,000 (US$144,700) loan was given.

The struggles to find outside financing are not unique to Sukau Rainforest Lodge. Many other ecotourism lodge owners have turned to their savings or friends and families for financing. A study done by Edward Sanders and Elizabeth Halpenny, titled The Business of Ecolodges, found that 58 per cent of owners used their own funds to finance their ecolodges. In developing countries, only 13 per cent were able to obtain bank or government loans. Clearly this is a huge obstacle business owners must overcome.

Just like "Discovery Channel" in real life but much better! Too bad that you can't get the sounds on a picture. An experience we never forget and very friendly and professional guides and staff.
Wibeke Pedersen and Martin Madsen, Marco Polo Tours, Denmark
16th February 2001

Wonderful nature! It was a privilege to share. We hope that more people like Borneo Eco Tours can learn to mix tourism with ecology so that our grandchildren can come here. Thank you for a lovely stay.
T. Stafford Allen, England
8th March 2001

Economic Impacts

The Lodge has grown to be a major employer in the Sukau area. It provides permanent employment for 15 full-time staff and work for five people on a part-time basis. Thirteen of the 15 full-time employees and all the part-time employees are from the local area. Albert realizes that his salaries may not be the highest in the region but still his employees are well compensated. "When a family member of a Lodge employee dies, the family often looks to the employee for help with burial costs as they realize our staff will likely have the money," he says, a reflection on how well regarded his staff are in their own community.

As mentioned in Chapter 4, SRL hired local people to assist in the Lodge construction, build boats, provide building materials, construct the jetty, drive some of the boats, and provide regular supplies of fish and prawns.

Overall, he estimates that the Lodge injected over RM 500,000 (US$131,600) into the local economy during the years 1995 to 1999. And on a current basis, the Lodge injects approximately RM150,000 (US$ 39,500) each year into the local economy through salaries, allowances, boat charters, and the purchase of fish and prawns.

Achieving Profitability

Readers will by now realize that an ecolodge faces some hard economic realities. Financing is hard to find, water and power systems require unique technology, involving the local community requires patience and long-term investment in labor pools. Occupancy rates are far lower than traditional accommodation providers might see. The Lodge will have an average occupancy rate of 35 per cent while conventional hoteliers will need occupancies in the range of 60 to 70 per cent to break-even. With other lodges in Sukau and Sabah competing with the Lodge for travelers, it is a constant struggle to maintain tour prices. Few consumers understand the concept of an ecolodge or are willing to pay a premium to cover additional operating costs.

All of these factors can make it difficult to achieve profitability. With Albert's previous experience in the hospitality industry and the ingenuity of his managers, Sukau Rainforest Lodge was able to reach a critical financial milestone. Partway through 1997 revenues exceeded expenses, meaning the Lodge had achieved break-even. Building on this success, the Lodge was able to make a small profit every year from 1997 until 2000. "This helped recoup the heavy losses of 1995 and 1996," he said.

But the Lodge is not immune to global events and the large downturn in tourism from 9/11, SARS and other problems resulted in losses for 2001, 2002 and 2003. He hopes that world economic and political conditions will improve and travel to Southeast Asia will rebound. The goal is to increase profits to improve the Lodge facilities and eventually repay the current loan, but Albert and his investors realize they are juggling a "triple bottom line" of economic, social and environmental measures. He sums it up best when he said, "The success of this Lodge will have to be measured not just from its bottom line or profitability, but also from its positive impact on the economic and social aspects of the local people through employment, as a change agent or catalyst on other tourism operators, its impact on the landscape through tree planting, and the long term impact on the tourists through education and involvement in local community projects. We believe everyone must be a winner from this ecolodge."

We thank you so much for the authentic, attentive and thoughtful services. Keep and maintain your excellent goals and services. May our good and Almighty GOD continue to give you strength, joy and peace to do His will for His glory. It was really a relaxing time to be here! Hope to be here again in the next year...
Maryln & Rainer Leyendecker, Germany
26th April 2002

It's a wonderful place. I've received more then I expected. Our guides-Herman & Fernando gave all the best to make this time even nicer. The best place in the world to stay for holidays. And all the animals-orangutans, elephants, birds, monkey. I hope to be here pretty soon.
Elzbieta Lzakowska, Poland
28th April 2002

Rufous Piculet

Tour Planning

"Man must cease attributing his problems to his environment, and learn again to exercise his will – his personal responsibility." Albert Schweitzer

As Sukau Rainforest Lodge was being completed, the need to develop tour itineraries that would showcase the best of the Kinabatangan river basin became obvious. The aim was to link together activities and customs that would convey the uniqueness of the region and help them fall in love with Sabah's wilderness.

The highlight of my visit to Borneo. More birds than I've seen elsewhere. I'm especially impressed with the dedication to conservation/eco-tourism. I hope other operators can take inspiration from you. Thanks!
Christina Liadis, Festival of Asia, San Francisco, USA
22nd November 1996

As most people want to see the monkeys, apes and birds of Borneo without the hardship of sleeping in primitive shelters or eating camping-style meals, the Lodge with its comfortable facilities gives an immediate advantage in tour planning. Communicating the level of comfort people would enjoy at the Lodge lets it target the type of customers who would be willing to pay more for comfort and increase the profitability of the business. "It is necessary to increase the length of stay and to attract the 'comfortable tourists' who are not the backpacking type and who are willing to pay for more comfort," Albert said.

Attracting this upmarket clientele would mean Sukau Rainforest Lodge must meet international levels of service. He sums up what would be a daunting task, "For our tour to be different and unique, we have to examine the whole delivery of our service from the type of transportation used, for example, by land or by water; the type of boat engines used; the size of boat used to maximize a sense of privacy; the type of lighting used to reduce insects and create a sense of ambience; and the interpretative materials whether they be slide shows, jungle walks or night cruises."

To create truly memorable tours, Lodge management carried forward the elements they had incorporated during the Lodge's design phase and added activities and services that would satisfy everyone from the most active traveller to people looking for more R&R. From the time visitors step onto the Lodge's jetty, they are given numerous activity choices. The Lodge has a fully stocked library, there are board games available, and most evenings there are slide shows and optional night cruises. Guests are also encouraged to move freely around the Lodge. There are several small decks, some covered, some open, giving visitors several places for watching wildlife, reading, or relaxing and contemplation. People wanting a bit more exercise can enjoy a walk around the 450 metre (1,500 feet) raised boardwalk. With guests coming from all over the world, there is always the opportunity for sharing experiences and meeting new friends.

Fantastic! We are in the middle of the jungle and this is a superb lodge with excellent accommodation, a relaxed atmosphere and staff who cannot do enough to make you feel welcome. And there is the wildlife. What more could anyone want? A few more days perhaps. Colin Mcdem, United Kingdom *6th August 1999*

Of course the real attraction for Lodge visitors is the boat cruises and the chance to get close to the wildlife. The electric motors make it possible to approach the animals without disturbing them and the well-trained guides always have a ready explanation of what the visitor is seeing. Guides have the option of taking the boats down several waterways and will vary their routes based upon where the wildlife has been most recently spotted.

Guests looking for more information on the Orang Sungai culture can visit Sukau village and stop at a local home for coffee which often will be offered very sweet. It is a sign of good manners and wealth of the host to serve sweet coffee. For people wanting the chance to actually walk in the rainforest, hikes are offered. Some of these have resulted in unexpected animal encounters. Neil Degullacion, a Lodge Guide, remembers one of his night walks with a group of guests. "Walking at night with tourists in the forest is a very unique experience. Sharing the unique habitats, the calling of the insects is a wonderful pleasure. Walking for two hours in the forest in the dark, sometimes your eyes play tricks on you. Stepping over a huge snake without actually realizing it is a scary moment. I was thinking it was just a fallen tree blocking the trail, just a normal thing. But after a trekker noticed it and we investigated, it turned out to be a close shave. The so-called fallen tree on the path was actually a reticulated python snake."

Although not every guest has this kind of excitement, all are able to see some of the region's 10 species of primates. "It really is the monkeys that make visitors fall in love with Sabah almost immediately without a word being spoken," says Albert. For most visitors they will follow an itinerary (see Suggested Itineraries) that gives them a variety of wildlife experiences.

Suggested Itineraries

Kinabatangan Wildlife Safari (3 days)
Day 1
On arrival at Sandakan airport by MH2129 ETA 8.50 am, proceed for a short tour of Sandakan town including a tea break in one of the houses on the water village and the Australian War Memorial. Continue to Sandakan jetty for an estimated two hour boat journey to Sukau Rainforest Lodge along Sabah's longest river, the Kinabatangan, with the opportunity to view birds and wildlife in virgin mangrove, wetland and rainforest habitats. Late afternoon take a two hour river cruise using electric motors in search of some of the 10 primate species including Proboscis monkeys as they settle down on treetops along the Kinabatangan River. Return for a solar-heated hot shower, candlelight dinner and slide show conducted by a naturalist guide. Overnight at Sukau Rainforest Lodge. **(LD)**

Day 2
Wake up to the calls of gibbons and hornbills. A 6.00 am morning river cruise up the Kinabatangan River to view more birds and wildlife. Proceed to the Kelenanap ox-bow lake for a short jungle walk (if weather permits). Experience the wilderness of Borneo. You have the option to participate in our conservation project by planting trees at our 64 acres of adopted land. After breakfast, transfer by boat to Sukau Village for a short tour.

In the afternoon, we proceed for another river cruise to look for more wild-life. After dinner an optional (at a surcharge) night safari cruise spotting nocturnal animals, crocodiles and birds. Overnight at Sukau Rainforest Lodge. **(BLD)**

Day 3
After breakfast return to Sandakan by boat journey. Lunch at Sandakan before proceeding to Sepilok Orang Utan Rehabilitation Centre. Trek ten minutes through the rainforest on wooden plank walks to witness the feeding of the Orang-utans at 3.00 pm and video show. Transfer to airport for departure flight MH2065 ETD 5.20pm. **(BL)**

Sabah Wildlife Safari **(7 days)**
Day 1   Kota Kinabalu
On arrival, transfer to your hotel. At sunset, drive up to Signal Hill for a bird's eye view of the city. Visit the colourful local night market before we go for a scrumptious dinner. **(D)**

Day 2   Gaya-Sapi Islands
After breakfast, transfer to jetty for a half-hour boat ride to Gaya Island . Put on your walking shoes and explore one of the jungle trails (45 minutes) among lowland rainforest, mangrove swamp and identify some unique floras and faunas. Transfer five minutes to Sapi Island for picnic lunch. Free at leisure to swim, snorkel or scuba dive before we transfer back to mainland and hotel. **(BL)**

Day 3   Kinabalu World Heritage Site - Poring
Drive 2 hours overland (88 km) through padi-fields and Dusun villages over the ridges of the Crocker Range to the foothills of Mt. Kinabalu at 5,000ft, to arrive at the park headquarters at Kundasang. Visit the Visitor Centre and Mountain Garden; home to some of the 24 species of flowering rhododendrons, 10 species of carnivorous pitcher plants, estimated 1,400 species of orchids, over 600 species of ferns, more than 40 species of oak trees and over 300 species of birds.

Continue 40 km journey to Poring. Explore tropical rainforest among the jungle trail leading to the treetop canopy walkways suspended 41 meters above the forest floor before returning to sea-level. **(BL)**

Day 4   Sandakan/Selingan
Transfer to airport for morning flight MH2129 ETD 8.00 am to Sandakan. On arrival at Sandakan airport ETA 8.50 am, transfer to jetty for 45 minutes boat ride by speedboat to Selingan Island (40km), fully equipped and licensed to carry 12 persons. Check into chalet. Free at leisure to explore island, swim and snorkel. After dinner, wait for signal from the Park Ranger before we proceed in small groups to watch Green Turtle lay eggs on the beach. This island is a park conservation area since 1977 and turtles have been nesting here every night throughout the year. Overnight in twin sharing room (with common bath). **(BLD)**

Photographing turtles is strictly prohibited between 6pm - 6am.

Day 5   Selingan/Sukau

Return to Sandakan by boat and proceed for a short tour of Sandakan town including a tea break in one of the houses on the water village and the Australian War Memorial. Continue to Sandakan jetty for an estimated 2 hours boat journey to Sukau Rainforest Lodge along Sabah's longest river, the Kinabatangan, with opportunity to view birds and wildlife in virgin mangrove, wetland and rainforest habitats. Late afternoon take a two hours river cruise using electric motor in search of some of the 10 primate species including Proboscis monkeys as they settle down on treetops along the Kinabatangan River. Return for solar-heated hot shower, candlelight dinner and slide show conducted by naturalist guide. Overnight at Sukau Rainforest Lodge. **(BLD)**

Day 6   Sukau

Wake up to the calls of gibbons and hornbills. A 6.00 am morning river cruise up the Kinabatangan River to view more birds and wildlife. Proceed to the Kelenanap ox-bow lake for a short jungle walk (if weather permits). Experience the wilderness of Borneo. You have the option to participate in our conservation project by planting trees at our 64 acres adopted land. After breakfast, transfer by boat to Sukau Village for a short tour. In the afternoon, we proceed for another river cruise for more wildlife. After dinner an optional (at a surcharge) night safari cruise spotting nocturnal animals, crocodiles and birds. Overnight at Sukau Rainforest Lodge. **(BLD)**

Day 7   Sukau/Sepilok

Return to Sandakan by boat journey. Lunch at Sandakan before proceed to Sepilok Orang Utan Rehabilitation Centre. Trek ten minutes through the rainforest on wooden plank walks to witness the feeding of the Orang-utans at 3.00 pm and video show. Transfer to airport for departure flight MH2065 ETD 5.20pm. **(BL)**

Visitors to the Lodge are also encouraged to participate in activities and customs that expose them more fully to the local community and culture. Visitors are invited to take their shoes off each time they come into the Lodge. In addition to a welcome drink and briefing by the manager, each guest will find a neatly folded 'sarong' on their bed on their arrival. While some may wonder in jest if this is the Malaysian equivalent of a bath robe, it is in fact their dinner attire. Guests are given a demonstration by one of the staff on how to wear this traditional Malaysian garment. Fastening it securely requires a little practice and visitors listen carefully lest their carelessness results in a loose sarong and some unexpected breezes at dinner! Visitors often find this custom a great ice-breaker with fellow guests and a chance to feel more connected to the Malaysian culture.

48 years as a Malaysian and I wore a sarong for the first time yesterday! Lovely place. Will definitely recommend local travel to my friends.
Suheele Sham, Kota Kinabalu
7th August 1999

The ecotourism practices of the Lodge are also woven throughout the visitor experience. Each guest will receive a copy of the Visitor Handbook on the Lower Kinabatangan Floodplain with "Guidelines for Ecotourists" and local flora and fauna to help them understand the unique features of the Lodge and how they can take steps that will reduce the environmental and social impacts of their travel. Some of the Lodge's environmental programs also encourage active guest participation. SRL's efforts to reforest land damaged by logging and agriculture mean that visitors get the chance to help in reforestation. Guests can help plant a tree seedling bought by the Lodge in what will hopefully become a new forest and provide valuable animal habitat. They can also make a personal contribution if they so wish towards the reforestation program.

A wide range of activities and a strong ecotourism philosophy are critical for an ecolodge's tour planning, but they will not be complete without a high level of customer service. Borneo Eco Tours and SRL go out of their way to teach their staff on how best to deliver quality service. They provide training on how to make beds, clean rooms, serve meals, and respond to guest requests. They also put in place control systems so that food inventories are kept at the correct level (more on this can be found in Chapter Eight.) Foreign hospitality students were invited to intern at the Lodge for periods of three to six months. These students helped staff overcome their shyness as they practised their English and were also instrumental in demonstrating the high levels of cleanliness needed in housekeeping practices.

Orang utan eating wild figs

Benjamin Golimbi, Manager of the Lodge in 1995, noticed how important the customer service improvements were. "As we improved the service of Sukau Rainforest Lodge by practising personalized service and service with a smile, I realized that it does make some impact towards our in-house guests. Many good comments were said and I always give credit to my fellow staff as they are the one that made all the things run smoothly," he said.

With a great tourism product in place, Lodge management turned its attention to getting the word out. Marketing strategies would be critical in achieving the financial goals. We will hear more about them in the next Chapter.

Guidelines for Ecotourists

When you are on tours......

Request a copy of your tour itinerary on your arrival. Read it carefully and discuss any questions with your guide as soon as possible. If something is incorrect, the earlier you mention it, the more likely it can be rectified.

Note departure times. Be punctual to avoid inconveniencing others. You may be the one who misses your flight!

Use vehicles that are licensed to carry tourists. These will have **Bas Persiaran** written on these vehicles. There are periodic road checks of these driving licenses. If you are in an unlicensed vehicle, you will be sitting at the check-point until a licensed vehicle and driver arrive.

Use coastal and river boats that are not overloaded and wear a life jacket. (Note: Not more than 12 people per boat.) Tourists are required by law to wear a life jacket in a boat.

Encourage drivers to stop engines when vehicles and boats are parked. The driver may start the car just before you enter on a hot day so that the air-conditioning can cool the vehicle for your comfort.

All tours must be guided by local Malaysian licensed guides who hold either a blue, green, or yellow badge. It is illegal for non-Malaysians to guide in the country but a non-Malaysian can be a translator.

Carry your identity papers or a copy of these papers with you. There are a number of occasions on which you may be asked for your passport. These include check-in at hotels, the climb up Mount Kinabalu, the boat trip to Sukau, and a road inspection for illegal residents.

Keep the place clean before you leave the area and carry out the litter for proper disposal. Leave nothing but footprints.

Always use the natural resources including water and energy efficiently.
Ask for permission if you want to take photographs of local people. Most people will smile and graciously say "yes"; some will say "no" because they are tired of having tourists take their picture; some may say "no" because it contravenes their beliefs. For example, I once asked a man if I could take his photo with a big fish he was about to kill. He was visibly upset by this and said "no". It has been explained to me that he is Buddhist and that they respect life. Hence he did not wish to be photographed with something that he was about to kill. If possible, send copies of photos to your subjects.

Dress sensibly. Skimpy clothing may be fine at your hotel pool, but it does not protect you from sunburn, skin cancer in later years, scratches in the forest, and insect bites. Sunscreen must be applied properly to prevent sunburn. It is still not known if sunscreen protects from skin cancer. Scratches and in-sect bites can easily become infected in the tropics. The best clothing is loose cotton clothing.... comfortable walking shoes, a hat, long-sleeved shirt, and long pants... and be prepared for rain. This is the rainforest.

Drink plenty of liquids, especially water. Bottled water is readily available. Carry a bottle with you so you do not become dehydrated. Do not wait until you are thirsty to drink. Heat exhaustion and heat stroke can be avoided by those not accustomed to the climate and/or suffering from jet-lag.

Respect the sensitivities of local people... There are accepted dress codes at certain places. As a matter of courtesy, please conform to these codes. At some places you may be provided with clothing to wear for certain events. Please comply with these requests. Remember while local people practise many different religious beliefs, this is a Muslim country. Most Muslim ladies dress modestly in public.

Take off shoes before entering a house. While this is a local tradition, it is also a means of keeping mud and animal droppings outside and floors inside clean.

Wear natural colours and avoid substances with perfumes. This will increase your opportunities to view wildlife in the rainforest.

On wildlife river tours, follow the directions of the guide when you are being seated in the boat. The guide is balancing the boat for your safety and maximum efficiency. Do not move suddenly and always check with your guide if you wish to stand for a better view or to take photos.

Stay on the trail to minimize damage to the surrounding area. If possible do not even leave footprints. Stay with your guide because it is very easy to get lost in the rainforest.

Be patient when viewing wildlife and give the animals plenty of space. You are less likely to cause alarm (in which case the animal may flee or attack) and be able to watch the animal behaving normally. Do not smoke in the forest or during wildlife viewing on river cruise.

Do not disturb, harass, or feed wildlife. Keep the noise level low.

Do not collect your own "souvenirs" from the rainforest. It is illegal to remove plants and animals from many of the areas that you are visiting without a special collecting permit. It is also illegal to transport many of these things internationally without a permit. Take only photographs and memories with you.

Abide by local regulations.

Support the local economy by buying locally made goods and foodstuff but do not buy items from endangered species. Also think which items you can take back to your home country. For example, wooden items may need to be fumigated so avoid disappointment by considering if you are willing to pay for fumigation and if the item is likely to be damaged. Many local people have given up their traditional hunting lifestyle in order to protect the wildlife in the remaining natural habitat. These people now need another way to earn a living because they now have to buy more food items.

Encourage or better still participate in the local conservation project such as tree planting to replace patches of trees illegally logged, or perhaps help a local charity such as a drive to provide books to the local school. The local people have been willing to share their world with you; a little help would be appreciated.

Notify your guide or other tour personnel if you are having a problem. For example, if the air-conditioning is not cooling the back of the vehicle, tell your guide. Perhaps the problem can be solved by a few minor adjustments; at worst the system can be fixed after the trip for the comfort of the next visitors.

When you return............

Provide feedback to a local operator, your travel agent, and a government agency. Borneo Eco Tours provides a guest comment form with every itinerary. The company acts on these comments, evaluates staff performance and provides staff with incentives and training based on your comments.

The following suggested list of items to bring, is in addition to the suggestions made on the previous pages and your "normal travel" gear.

Things to Bring:
Hat
Raincoat or poncho
Sunscreen
Insect repellent (products containing DEET will also repel leeches)
Absorbent body powder (some travelers suffer from prickly heat)
Leech socks (available on request)
Torch with good batteries
Passport and visa

The following is a good idea also:
Binoculars
Camera with ASA 400 film
Medical Information:
    Immunisation Record.
    Blood type
    Health alerts (e.g. diabetic)
    Allergies to medication (e.g. penicillin)

Please inform the staff of any special dietary requirements in advance of meals.

Orang Utans on a lone standing tree

Scarlet-rumped Tragon

Chapter Seven

Niche Marketing

"The aim of marketing is to know and understand the customer so well the product or service fits him and sells itself." Peter F. Drucker

Albert Teo understood his potential customers from the many years he worked in the hospitality and tour business and was in a good position to market Sukau Rainforest Lodge.   He created his own tour company, Borneo Eco Tours (BET), in 1991 and specialized in nature, adventure and cultural tours of Borneo (see 'Borneo Eco Tours'). His market research at BET and the time he took to solicit customer comments had given him a solid understanding of what customers were looking for and who was likely to visit Sukau Rainforest Lodge.

Borneo Eco Tours

Borneo Eco Tours Sdn. Bhd. (BET) was set up in 1991. BET specializes in ecotourism tours in Borneo. Some of the activities they offer include cultural tours, nature exploration, photography, and adventure sports such as white-water rafting, hiking, and diving. It had a total of 43 staff in 2004.

BET has offices in Kota Kinabalu, Sandakan and Sukau. It has a fleet of 17 vehicles including several coaches, mini-vans, limousine cars and land cruisers. It has also five speedboats for transfers from Sandakan to Turtle Island Park and Sukau Rainforest Lodge, and five 'perahu', the small wooden boats used for river tours.

Our Vision
To make Borneo Eco Tours a No. 1 service provider through passion for excellence in our work by developing the leadership potential of our staff, commitment to integrity, good attitude, and concern for the community and environment.
1. Make our company a No. 1 service provider – **commitment**
2. through passion for excellence – **consistent**
3. developing the leadership potential of our staff – **competence**
4. commitment to integrity, good attitude – **character**
5. concern for the community and environment - **cohesion**

He felt the Lodge would appeal to "the tourists who want to learn and experience what it is to stay in the rainforest; who want to see the wildlife of Borneo such as Orang-utans, macaques and Proboscis monkeys; and who want comfort, good meals and a high standard of service and reliability." He knew it was important to market the Lodge itself to nature lovers. "The Lodge ensures maximum guest satisfaction throughout the holiday experience, particularly in remote areas where accommodation facilities and services may be lacking. A good lodge gives us the competitive edge and distinctive image for special interest groups," Albert said. "We were using another lodge before 1995, but due to the lack of service consistency, the foods served and the 'pinching' of our customer base, we had to develop our own lodge to cater strictly to our own philosophy."

Albert knew the ecolodge would be more successful if marketed to countries where people were familiar with and supportive of the concept of ecotourism. He targeted potential customers in North America, Europe, Australia, and to a lesser extent, Asia. This strategy has proved successful. The composition of visitors change from year to year, but on average 80 per cent come from North America, Europe and Australia. Twenty per cent are local visitors or from other countries in Asia although this figure is increasing as more people become aware of ecotourism and the Lodge. BET is seeing more bookings from professionals, ecotourism devotees, and expatriates living in Japan, Singapore, Brunei and China, as the economy improves in these countries and as people in the middle and upper classes look for authentic, nature-based travel experiences.

> Excellent! This place is exactly how all travel agencies should be. Borneo Eco Tours is setting an example to the rest of the world. The staff is exceptional. Thank you.
> *Marnie and Richard Rose, Brunei*
> 20th May 1996

Research done by BET and the Lodge show there are distinct market segments attracted to the Lodge. For those fully-independent travelers, known as FITs in the industry, the typical tourist is likely to be in the 30 to 40 age range, equally likely to be married or single, makes their own travel arrangements through the Internet, and looks to stay in Borneo at least seven to 10 days. They are great wildlife lovers and will often combine a stay at the Lodge with other nature attractions such as Sepilok Orang Utan Rehabilitation Centre, Tunku Abdul Rahman Park and Kinabalu Park.

People traveling to the Lodge with an organized group have slightly different demographics and tastes. These group travelers are more likely to come from Europe or the United States and are somewhat older than FITs, with ages ranging from 55 to 75 years. They will usually stay for one or two weeks and are likely to include Danum Valley in their plans so they can see virgin rainforest and the wildlife found there. Most of these group travelers are on a tour affiliated with a zoo or museum; often these people are financial supporters of conservation efforts and belong to groups such as WWF.

> An Orang-utan the first morning, a 4-metre python the last night, 5 species of hornbills sandwiched in between. Just a wonderful three days. On top of all the birds and wildlife, we made new friends, ate well and laughed a lot. You've done a wonderful job, and we wish you well with your mission to bring ECOTOURISM to Borneo and benefit local people. This is such a fragile environment. We know you will steward it well. Best of luck.
> *Tom & Jeanne Joseph, Asia Transpacific Journeys, USA*
> 3rd April 2000

Marketing Strategies

Sukau Rainforest Lodge is marketed and packaged by its sister company Borneo Eco Tours. BET will combine Lodge stays with other attractions and lodges to give visitors tours of one to 14 days duration (see Sample Itinerary – River and Rainforest). Having a diverse menu of itineraries allows BET to market the Lodge to different market segments, from thrill seekers to education tourists, to honeymooners, and more.

BET employs a variety of marketing strategies to attract Lodge customers. For example, to encourage domestic visitors, a large discount of approximately 60 per cent is offered to Malaysian guests on a three-day package subject to room availability. BET also work to increase brand awareness of the Lodge by participating in a variety of media opportunities such as creating video productions, publishing travel books, hosting travel writers, and speaking at conferences around the world including New York, Japan, Taiwan, Bali and Fiji, and at trade shows in London and Berlin among others.

BET is also part of a cooperative marketing partnership with other lodges. This group has a separate brand name, Classic Lodges, and is attracting tourists looking for a holiday with stays at multiple locations, something one lodge cannot provide.

Sample Itinerary - River and Rainforest (5 days)

Day 1   Sandakan/Sepilok/Sukau Rainforest Lodge

On arrival at Sandakan airport by MH2042 at 7.40 am, transfer to Sepilok Rehabilitation Centre. Trek ten minutes through the rainforest on wooden plankwalks to witness the feeding of the Orang-utans at 10.00am. Continue to Sandakan jetty for an estimated two-hour boat journey to Sukau Rainforest Lodge along Sabah's longest river, the Kinabatangan, with the opportunity to view birds and wildlife in virgin mangrove, wetland and rainforest habitats. Late afternoon take a two-hour river cruise using electric motors in search of some of the 10 primate species including Proboscis monkeys as they settle down on treetops along the Kinabatangan River. Return for a solar-heated hot shower, candlelight dinner and slide show conducted by naturalist guide. Overnight at Sukau Rainforest Lodge. **(LD)**

Day 2   Sukau

Wake up to the calls of gibbons and hornbills. A 6.00 am morning river cruise up the Kinabatangan River to view more birds and wildlife. Proceed to the Kelenanap ox-bow lake for a short jungle walk (if weather permits). Experience the wilderness of Borneo. You have the option to participate in our conservation project by planting trees at our 64 acres adopted land. After breakfast, transfer by boat to Sukau Village for a short tour. In the afternoon, we proceed for another river cruise for more wildlife. After dinner an optional (at a surcharge) night safari cruise spotting nocturnal animals, crocodiles and birds. Overnight at Sukau Rainforest Lodge. **(BLD)**

Day 3   Sukau/Gomantong/Borneo Rainforest Lodge

Proceed 27 km overland to Gomantong Caves. Trek 20 minutes through the rainforest to the cave entrance. Your guide will brief you on the cave faunas including bats, swiftlets and crabs among others and their contribution to maintaining a balanced ecology and significance to the local economy. When in season, witness the collecting of birds' nests by the local people using bamboo ladders and poles.

Proceed two hours overland to Lahad Datu for lunch. Drive 83km through selectively-logged forest, cocoa and soft-wood plantations before arriving at the Borneo Rainforest Lodge beside Danum River on the edge of 438 sq. km of undisturbed lowland rainforest. The lodge is home to the full range of Sabah's lowland fauna, including the rare Sumatran Rhinoceros, Elephants, Clouded Leopards, and Orang-utans. So far some 275 species of birds have been recorded in the area. Explore nature trail and nearby river. In the evening a slide show and if weather permits one can go spotlighting to view some of the nocturnal animals. Overnight at Borneo Rainforest Lodge.**(BLD)**

Day 4   Borneo Rainforest Lodge
Early morning bird watching walk before breakfast. Spend the whole day exploring the forest for birds and mammals, leading up to an escarpment with ancient burial coffins. Trek to waterfall and dip in refreshing rock pools. Lunch at the lodge. In the afternoon, take a jungle walk through trails leading to a canopy walkway. Overnight at Borneo Rainforest Lodge. **(BLD)**

Day 5   Transfer out
Morning trek in search of mammals and birds. Return to the Centre for lunch before departing for Lahad Datu. Take the last flight MH2097 5.35 pm/6.30 pm to Kota Kinabalu. **(BL)**

Marketing Activities

BET, on behalf of the Lodge, uses a variety of marketing methods to advertise. They produce a printed brochure which is updated every two years. This brochure is distributed at travel shows or mailed in response to tourist enquiries. Attendance at major travel shows is important in building a customer base in Europe and North America. BET attends the World Travel Mart (WTM) in London, ITB in Berlin and the Asean Tourism Forum (ATF) among others. These shows put BET and Sukau Rainforest Lodge in touch with consumers, and with travel wholesalers who will add the Lodge to the packages they sell through travel agents.

The Internet has become increasingly important in marketing the Lodge. Through BET's website at http://www.borneoecotours.com and SRL website at http://www.sukau.com travelers can book their own travel arrangements for a holiday in Borneo. "The Lodge is increasingly attracting ecotourists from more diverse countries through the Internet," says Albert. The use of the world-wide web has allowed BET to reach customers in countries that were not traditional markets for them; and it also has been helpful in recent years when global events have made customers more safety conscious and likely to wait until the last minute to book vacations. He has noticed some positive trends come out of this situation as some customers have been choosing Borneo, perceived as a safer destination, as they alter their holiday plans in response to travel advisories.

Superb! Beautiful setting, very hospitable staff, wish I could've stayed longer, very refreshing to see ecotourism in practice – not just as a marketing ploy – GREAT!
Adele Mova, United Kingdom
21st May 2003

Albert is an accomplished photographer and uses his pictures to create travel books (see Books by Albert Teo) and postcards. He has also turned his photos into a set of bookmarks which include inspirational quotes from some of the world's most profound thinkers. The books, postcards and bookmarks help to market Borneo and the Lodge. The postcards and bookmarks are extremely portable and send images of this nature lover's destination around the world as they are exchanged.

> ## Books by Albert Teo
>
> Sabah – Land of the Sacred Mountain (1988)
> Exotic Islands of Tunku Abdul Rahman Park (1989)
> A Guide to Sandakan (1990)
> A Guide to Brunei Darussalam (1992)
> Journey through Borneo (1994)
> Images of Borneo (1996)

Pricing

Management has struggled with how to price tour packages for tourists staying at the Lodge. Most visitors pay an all-inclusive fee that includes accommodation, meals, river cruises and nature walks. With five other lodges in the Sukau area, there is stiff price competition. Some of these tour operators charge 10 to 30 per cent less than the Lodge. With its higher operating costs and commitment to conservation projects, the Lodge must compete on quality to survive. Unfortunately few tourists understand ecotourism or make their choice of one lodge over another based on a commitment to conservation. In the Lodge's early years, Albert observed that "At present, ecotourism holidays are not in high demand. Hence the high cost of tour operations where there is more importance placed on environmental protection and these costs are borne by a relatively small number of tourists." As the main customer base for the Lodge is the up-market tourist who is informed on the environmental issues, the overall market size is small, and there are few economies of scale to offset the higher cost structure.

The Lodge has reacted to these challenges by focusing on value instead of price (see "Ecotourism Myths"). It include activities that are unique, such as the night cruises or the opportunity to take part in a conservation project, and uses BET's extensive fleet of boats and vehicles to include quick and hassle-free transfers from Sandakan up the Kinabatangan River as part of each tour experience.

> ### Ecotourism Myths
>
> 1. People tend to think that ecotourism is for the adventurous and the fit. This is not so. We put more emphasis on interpretation, personal encounters with nature, quality of tour, value for money and minimum environmental impact.
> 2. There is no money in ecotourism. This is not so. Travel agents tend to focus too much on price and overlook the importance of value for money and the needs of the customers.
> 3. We often hear the same price quoted for a quality product and presentation, but travel agents often do not bother to emphasise the benefits and differences of eco-tours to customers.

Repeat Visitors and New Markets

Visitors are always impressed by the beauty of the Kinabatangan river basin and the warmth of the Lodge staff. Some of them return time after time, with approximately five per cent of visitors returning more than once. In addition to maintaining the highest standards of customer service, SRL is working to increase the number of repeat tourists by increasing the facilities and diversifying the type of accommodation provided by the Lodge. This expansion which will include individual cottages will also allow BET to market to customers who may be seeking greater luxury or privacy than the current facilities provide.

By 2005, visitors will be able to stay in these individual cottages. The cottages will adhere to ecotourism principles for design and construction, and be more spacious and secluded than a Lodge room. The cottages will be connected to the Lodge by the raised boardwalk and allow visitors to access the main Lodge and its facilities. Albert feels this will be very attractive to "those tourists who demand more space, privacy and comfort, or want a longer stay."

Stork billed kingfisher

Common kingfisher

Spectacled Spiderhunter

Manpower Development

"In our interdependent world, you can't afford to let people lose out in pursuit of a decent life. Everyone must be a winner."
Professor Klaus Schwab for Newsweek, January 31, 2000.

Every business owner knows that employees are the most important resource. Tourists will remember the time with their guides and their experiences with Lodge staff as much as the wildlife watching. Having reliable, enthusiastic people willing and able to deliver great customer service was one of the Lodge's goals from the beginning. "It requires an investment of time and effort, but I have made it a company policy to train local people," Albert says.

The early days were a challenge as there were few qualified staff in the local area and those that were hired required a lot of training in hospitality skills and English. One of the early managers, Adrian Migiu, recalls the start-up period, "I remember vividly the early days of Sukau Rainforest Lodge where we only had six staff including myself to run the entire Lodge. Every one of the staff had to multitask. Each staff had to do housekeeping, boating, gardening, watering, guiding and entertaining the guests. We did not complain of the long hours that we put in. We were like a family unit and the guests were just impressed with us although some of us couldn't even speak proper English to them. I guessed partly because of all that, it helped to mould us to be persistent in our work and not easily give up when encountering problems. It was really an Outward Bound school experience in the true sense that it helped build character."

Even though these early days seemed a little hectic at times, Albert had a long-term vision for the type of people he would need at the Lodge and the skills they would require. He was not a newcomer to the hospitality industry when he built the Lodge. He had many years experience as an hotelier and a guide himself (see 'The Man Behind Sukau Rainforest Lodge'). But he knew he would need innovative processes for recruiting, training, and retaining staff that would take into account the Lodge's remote location and its commitment to ecotourism principles. Wherever possible, he wanted to hire local people and he had promised Kari, the original land owner, he would give preference to his relatives, but it would not be a simple process. The Orang Sungai did not have experience in the hospitality industry and English was not commonly spoken in the community. Many prospective employees were not interested in a job that required long hours for basic pay even though they did not have the training to get better-paying jobs.

The Man Behind Sukau Rainforest Lodge

Albert is an economist by education and has been an hotelier and tour operator since 1977. In 1986 Albert joined a tour company that specialized in tours of Sabah. That same year he learned to take pictures. "How can I promote Sabah without pictures? Buying other people's slides would be too expensive, and besides, they may not be relevant," he said. This was the practical start to a love affair with photography that resulted in several popular travel books by Albert.

In 1991, Albert wanted more independence and the ability to fully develop his interest in ecotourism, so he created his own tour company, Borneo Eco Tours. Sukau Rainforest Lodge was built in 1995 and he has new plans for a water-based eco-resort in the near future.

Albert has held many leadership positions in the tourism industry including Chairman of Sabah Tourist Association (1985/86), Chairman of Malaysian Association of Tour and Travel Agents (MATTA), Sabah Chapter (1991, 1996- 2001) and member of The International Ecotourism Society's Advisory Board (1996-2004). He also organised two international ecotourism conferences in Malaysia, one in 1999 and the other in 2002.

Albert enjoys spending time exploring Malaysia's natural wonders and has trekked more than 1,000 km in Sabah, Sarawak and Brunei.

The Lodge started by offering employment to Kari's relatives and those people who lived close to the Lodge. The Lodge manager and assistant manager are asked to interview potential candidates and make hiring choices in consultation with Albert and his General Manager/Director, Baton Bijamin. Now the managers increase hiring success by recruiting junior staff for part-time employment where it is possible to assess their ability, attitude and performance on the job. If they meet the Lodge requirements, they are hired as full-time staff.

Training of staff is an on-going process at the Lodge. To increase the levels of English spoken, students from hospitality schools in Europe and America have been invited to spend several months at the Lodge demonstrating proper hospitality processes and speaking English with the staff. Evening classes in English are offered to increase conversational and grammar skills, but the staff can still be shy about using their English with customers and Albert constantly encourages his people to mingle. Joseph Chong, a chef and later, Assistant Manager, remembers his efforts to speak English, "After cooking meals, I would always come out from the kitchen to entertain the guests. When I first started working for this company, my English was bad but I tried my best to learn and talk to the guests. I learnt a lot from the guests themselves."

Joseph Chong

Employees are also encouraged to participate in the Lodge's book reading program to cultivate the habit of reading and to improve their language skills. Those staff who read enough books to reach a book reading quota established by the manager are given free books. This program has a special place in Albert's heart. He hopes, "that by encouraging regular reading, it will cultivate the habit of personal development."

I am impressed by your staff who have kept the place so well.
Keep up the good work!
Francis Liew, Deputy Director, Sabah Parks, Malaysia
7th March 1998

The Lodge manager is responsible for training the staff in the daily tasks they need on the job. Since the Lodge opened in 1995, the senior guide from Borneo Eco Tours has been seconded for this position although local staff are taking on more and more senior roles as they have gained experience and competency in English.

In the early days, dealing with staff turnover was one of the Manager's bigger challenges. Staff recruited from the local community were not used to fixed hours of work and often resigned without notice. There were also problems with inventory loss and abuse. "Garden tools went missing; drinks for guests were consumed by 'elders' who were also relatives of the staff. Kitchen foods from ketchup to rice were pilfered by various ingenious means including making frequent trips home for no obvious reason or floating things in covered containers downriver," Albert explained. Some of these problems arose from differences in cultural values. In the Orang Sungai culture people with food or other commodities will share with other family or village members who may be lacking. Although he was sensitive to local customs, Management needed to minimize losses to ensure the Lodge's survival. Several steps were taken to control inventories including locking up the fridge, not over ordering stocks, regular stock counts, and petty cash control.

Benjamin Denis, remembers clearly the challenges in putting these processes in place, "There was no system at all when I took over as Lodge Manager. Almost everyone had access to everything at the Lodge. Not to mention that the former land owner and his family who at anytime would come and take anything they needed such as rice, sugar, coffee, and the list is long. So a sack of 60kg of rice would be finished with or without tourists within a week! It was not long after that I studied the situation and started implementing a system that would prevent this from happening. The response was bad and I started to experience backlash. The situation became so tense that whenever I started a new system, Mr. Kari would know and send his loyal sons to look for me with threats! Had it not been for the advice of Mr. Amad (father of a lodge worker), I would not have had the courage to go through all the turbulences." Benjamin was eventually able to resolve the tensions with the local residents. He made an effort to understand their point of view and to share with them the problems he faced as a Lodge employee; some of the most fruitful conversations occurred over libations. One time when Kari was quite angry over a perceived injustice, he arrived at the Lodge with a machete. Using diplomacy and hospitality, Benjamin offered Kari a beverage and they began to talk. They were able to resolve that situation and Benjamin gained a new insight into his neighbour, "I guess that this was the time that I really got the chance to understand him from a different perspective."

Fabulous! Perfect organisation!
Jan Lillieskold, President, Holiday Tours, Stockholm, Sweden
27th September 1995

We wish to extend our most sincere compliments to Borneo Eco Tours for the magnificent organization. This journey has fulfilled all our expectations to have an encounter with nature; especially this type of ecology which is not easy to experience for the ordinary traveller.
Esteban and Florence, Pzulin, Mexico
25th October 1995

Good place with bright future. Dedicated staff. Best wishes!
Leela Govindasamy, Editor, Selamat Datang, Malaysia
26th May 1995

Albert, as the final authority on the Lodge's operations, has been actively involved in its operations from the beginning. In the early days, he made monthly visits to check on operations, resolve problems, and spend time with the local residents. On these visits, he encounters the typical grievances and problems that an hotelier would normally see, plus a few that are unique to an ecolodge. On one trip he was somewhat dismayed to see his prized gardens had been trimmed almost to the ground. One of the staff members in his enthusiasm to present well-maintained grounds overlooked the fact that an ecolodge is a place to showcase different forms of vegetation, not trim them out of existence! In another instance, he got a major surprise when he made his usual rounds of the Lodge to see that all the potted "palm" plants had been heavily trimmed, leaving only the stalks and stems. When asked to trim the potted plants around the Lodge by the manager, the staff had obediently trimmed all the palms, but they removed all the leaves and left only the stems. Albert said, "Was the excess trimming of the plants due to cultural differences? It took me several months to figure out that there was a valuable lesson to be learnt here. The instructions that I think are clear can be confusing to someone with a different cultural background. I am now reminded each time I visit the Lodge and see the potted palms to be conscious of the other person's perspective."

The close relationship of the Lodge managers and staff with the community at Sukau has also meant that he is asked to referee in personal disputes with mother-in laws, respond to a demand by an uncle to remove a nephew from the staff payroll, or deal with black magic curses. "Sometimes they even come to see the Lodge manager with their jungle knives hoping to settle some grievances," Albert says. These visits have given him the chance to learn more about his neighbours, and provide ideas for the community projects that are an important part of Sukau Rainforest Lodge. These projects are discussed more in the next Chapter.

Joseph Chong with local naturalist guides Jamil and Sugiman

Guide Training

For many Lodge visitors, their lasting impressions will come from the experiences they share with their guide. A rare sighting, perhaps a palm civet cat, a funny story on someone's misadventures, or extra care for a guest's bad back on a long boat ride, are the things a customer remembers and shares with their friends back home. The Lodge's guides receive training as part of the State's guide training program.

The course syllabus is set by the Ministry of Culture, Arts and Tourism (MOCAT) and training is conducted by licensed tourism institutions. There are two levels of guide certification, Green badges and the higher level Blue badges. To obtain a Green badge, guides must have a Primary Six education, take a six-week course, and pass a final examination. This badge allows people to guide within a certain locality.

Those people wanting to obtain a Blue badge must have at least Form Five (Grade Three). They must also take a more extensive course and pass the final examination. Guides holding the Blue badge are permitted to guide anywhere in Malaysia. This two-tier system allows people with less education and fewer employment prospects to secure a guide's job in rural areas with ecotourism potential.

The Lodge supplements this guide training program with ongoing professional development. In addition to the reading program mentioned earlier, guides are encouraged to watch training and management videos, and participate in community or environmental projects. They are also given the opportunity to earn extra income by leading optional tours such as the night cruises as their language and communication skills improve.

Staff of Sukau Rainforest Lodge

In keeping with ecotourism principles, the Lodge encourages staff from the local area to move beyond junior positions, and gain the experience and training needed to become guides. Six years after the Lodge opened, Albert was able to announce that three Orang Sungai staff had completed the Green badge program, Herman Bin Abang, Jaini Amad, and Sugiman Sugiat. These guides received scholarships from Sukau Ecotourism Research & Development Centre (SERDC) of RM6,167 (US$1,600) to cover the costs of their three-week course in Kota Kinabalu. More staff have graduated since then. Sukau Rainforest Lodge sets aside US$1 per international tourist for SERDC's various projects. More information on SERDC and its programs is provided in later Chapters.

I have worked in the Nature-based tourism industry in Northern Australia for over seven years and have never had such service and enjoyment as I have had here at Sukau Rainforest Lodge. Every meal is a feast! Every trip is a new and refreshing natural history wonder. Your guides could work with me anytime.
Craig Brennan, Expert Touring Adventures, Darwin, Australia
28th January 1998

This lodge is very impressive. It is very well managed and most comfortable. I have been running quality nature-based tours in Northern Australia for 12 years now and I recognize a professional operation when I see one! Sukau Rainforest Lodge fits the bill! Elmo is certainly one of the best naturalist guides I have met – he is of international standard. The boat trip with him was very pleasant and informative and he employed all the Best Practices guiding skills, so ensuring that we had excellent opportunities to observe the animals in detail. Well done and congratulations to Mr. Teo for his achievements in sustainable nature tourism.
Rick Murray, Director/Operations, Odyssey Safaris, and President of Tourism Council Australia, NT Branch, Darwin, Australia
24th January 1999

Congratulations Joseph and all the staff for giving us such a memorable 2 days. The food was excellent and all the staff were very friendly and helpful. A special thanks to Herman, (he was brilliant), and we saw many, many animals, birds and amphibians, thanks to him. The elephants outside our room in the night were a highlight! Thank you all again and well done!
Kate and Oliver Halliwell, England
17th June 2001

Staff Retention

Staff turnover is a common problem in the hospitality industry. In a remote location like Sukau it can be even harder to retain good staff as recreational opportunities are limited and people may be separated from their families. As people have gained a greater understanding of the tourism industry and the Sukau community receives social and economic benefits from the Lodge, attitudes have changed. There is less resistance from parents to having their daughters return from Sandakan to work in the tourism industry in Sukau; and several staff members are making the effort to obtain their Green badges for guiding, a sign they plan to stay in the tourism industry. English levels of new recruits are also improving.

Although there were some problems in the start-up phase, Management is now satisfied with the current level of turnover. The average length of stay for junior staff is one to two years and five years for senior staff. Considerable effort is made to retain Lodge staff. They receive free accommodation and meals, and share in tips and service charges on guest beverages. The opportunity to live at the Lodge is well-received. Some staff prefer to stay at the Lodge even though they live nearby. Those staff who are recognized for their excellent customer service by being named in the guest feedback forms are given extra cash incentives. Each year Lodge employees are invited to a BET staff party in Kota Kinabalu where they are given the chance to visit major hotels and other tourist attractions to learn more about the travel industry. Staff are encouraged to develop regular savings habits to prepare for family emergencies such as funerals, and to undertake regular personal development such as participating in the Lodge's reading program.

Two managers from the Lodge join other BET managers from Sandakan and Kota Kinabalu for fortnightly meetings and training sessions with Albert. These leadership and personal development training programs are important in increasing skill and motivation levels for the managers and their staff. Reading and video materials are also given to the managers to use for training at the local level. Joseph Chong, Assistant Lodge Manager, comments on what this training meant to him, "I've enjoyed working with Sukau Rainforest Lodge because I can meet a lot of people from different countries and at the same time learn different languages. The company also organizes leadership courses and encourages the staff to read to improve our knowledge and to learn English for better communication with the guests." Through the meetings, videos, courses and financial incentives, the Lodge has created a culture of learning that encourages staff to become the best of their profession. Neil Dugullacion, a long-time employee, sums it up, "As a guide I must work hard and follow all the guidelines that have been prepared and must educate oneself to produce the best results of one's doing. Change comes and one must adapt and working with BET has helped me prepare for all these things. Be No. 1 with Borneo Eco Tours."

Had a great stay! Saw heaps of animals doing their thing. Loved the food and service too! Glad to see the use of solar power and water conservation. Good on you.
Lisa Dear, Deep Discoveries, Canada
8th February 2001

I stayed a bit longer than most and have been guided by almost all of the SRL staff. I am amazed by their absolute coordination and sharing of duties. They work and live as a big happy family. Who said the animals in the rainforest are difficult to see? Come to SRL and he'll be quickly proven wrong. Thank you everybody.
Henry Coleman, Borneo Magazine, Sabah
18th May 1996

These two days here were the best of our whole trip in Malaysia. You all are really wonderful and the food also. Our compliments to the cooks and also to the excellent waiters and guides.
Silvia Lucarini and Elisabeth Luciano, Prato, Italy
25th August 1996

Wonderful staff is a perfect complement to the spectacular nature and wildlife. Thanks for making us feel at home.
Richard Haas Winkelman, World Travel Consultants, USA
9th September 1996

Students of Royal College, UK at the weed clearing project (1996)

Stamford College students pose with the Minister of Tourism, YB Datuk Bernard Dompok after receiving their certificates for participating in the weed-clearing project (1996)

Stork-billed Kingfisher

Community and Environment Projects

Chapter Nine

If your vision is for a year, plant wheat.
If your vision is for ten years, plant trees.
If your vision is for a lifetime, plant people.
Chinese Proverb

"Many say it is not our responsibility, but I believe we need to take an interest in the local community and to share the benefits of ecotourism with them," so says Albert Teo. From the beginning, Albert knew that Sukau Rainforest Lodge could play an important role in the lives of local people. He did not want to create an 'enclave' resort with high fences that kept the community out and visitors isolated from the region they came to see. The design and construction of the Lodge aimed to minimize environmental degradation and wherever possible provided local economic benefits. This was consistent with ecotourism principles, but he knew more steps would be needed if the Lodge was to move beyond principles and truly make a difference in the lives of villagers. He envisioned a series of projects beyond the normal operations of the Lodge that would support conservation activities and improve the quality of life for the Orang Sungai people.

Weed Clearing Project

The earliest of these projects was started soon after the Lodge opened. It was an attempt to clean up a local oxbow lake, Kelenanap Lake, that had become covered with weeds in the early 1990s. The weeds are water hyacinth and *Salvinia molesta*, a very problematic non-native species introduced from Brazil. "No one knows the cause of the problem. It cannot have been caused by tourism though, as very few tourists visit the area," Albert said. The lake is more than six feet deep and isolated as no water appears to enter or leave the lake. The rapid growth of these weeds was preventing local people from fishing on the lake and was harming fish stocks and mammals such as otters. Some creative solutions were proposed for removing the weeds, such as introducing sterilized beetles to eat the roots of the weeds, but he took a more practical approach. He set aside 1,000 free room-nights at Sukau Rainforest Lodge for people who would volunteer to come and clear the weeds by hand-pulling. Borneo Eco Tours and the Lodge also contributed T-shirts, certificates, local transportation and logistical support. The Minister of Tourism and Environmental Development YB Datuk Bernard Dompok launched the program during the official opening of the Lodge in 1996. Five groups of volunteers came to the Lodge for this project, two of them traveling all the way from England. While not entirely successful in stopping the weeds, the project did achieve a measure of success in that it raised awareness at the local and international level of the negative impacts of introduced species.

Bavangazzo Longhouse

Although the persistent *Salvinia molesta* won round one, Albert kept at his efforts to support conservation and community-based projects. In 1996 and 1997 he was asked to advise another indigenous community, the Rungus people in Kudat, some 120 kilometers from Kota Kinabalu. The Rungus have opened the Bavangazzo Longhouse to overnight and day tourists wanting to experience the traditional Rungus lifestyle, but tourist numbers were low and the facility was not reaching its potential.

The Rungus hoped that Albert's experience at the Sukau Rainforest Lodge would help them improve their longhouse and its tourism program. He agreed to assist and a number of changes were implemented such as new marketing materials, changes to guest rooms and communal areas to improve visitor comfort, and staff training. Several members of the co-operative who managed the Longhouse were brought to Sukau for exposure. The Chairman was also invited to go with him for an educational visit to the Iban longhouse in Sarawak to observe how they operate their tourism accommodation. Later he was again asked to help the Rungus people, this time at Mompilis, by a charitable organization, the World Challenge of the United Kingdom. He put together a project for a school group to clean up the area around the Rungus longhouse at Mompilis, a facility also open to tourists. The community needed help in breaking the litter habit and were very appreciative of the time the students spent on the project and for his guidance.

Wildlife Rehabilitation

Back at Sukau, the Lodge staff wanted to rehabilitate wildlife that had minor injuries. In 1997 one of the staff rescued a young Buffy Fish owl with a broken leg. He was able to nurse it back to health in the staff quarters. The owl came to be known affectionately as 'Stingky' and was released when it was clear the owl could take care of itself. Stingky became a special 'bird friend' of Joseph, the Lodge's Assistant Manager. Joseph had a soft spot for Stingky and spoiled her with her favourite food whenever she showed up during dinner time. At one stage Stingky was not seen for months around the Lodge, but then the villagers in Sukau reported seeing an owl hanging around and stealing their little chicks. Realising it was Stingky and the difficult injury this bird had overcome, the villagers also developed a fondness for the bird. Stingky stills returns to the Lodge occasionally and one suspects it is out of gratitude and to say hello to Joseph.

Stingky, the buffy fish owl was among a few birds rehabilitated at the Lodge (1997)

With Stingky's successful rehabilitation to encourage them, the staff took in other animals needing help. Over the years with the support of the Wildlife Department, Lodge staff rehabilitated a pangolin, a rhinoceros hornbill and two pied hornbills. All of these were released into the forest behind the Lodge.

Our great thanks for the sensation of real coexistence with nature. We've been beautifully shocked by all that we've seen and the great part of the pleasant impression is due to the staff of the company. Our special thanks.
Serguei Gromozdine and Kalinitchev, Moscow, Russia
21st February 1998

It was very nice for us, and we hope that the nature will be there forever.
Harle Eva and Wendl Herbert, Pineapple Tours, Austria
23rd July 1998

It was a very exciting and pleasant experience. Most of all we had time to relax between cruises. We did three cruises in 3 days/2 nights and every time it was different. Keep the "eco" spirit above all!!
John Jourdan, via Internet from Belgium/Hong Kong
7th August 1998

Sukau Water Tank Project

One of SRL's most successful community initiatives was the water tank project launched in 1997. It started as an offshoot to the Lodge's practice of hiring local people to generate economic benefits. "Because we can only employ so many people we have started doing other things to help, such as donating rainwater tanks to the families nearby," Albert said. He felt these tanks could make a major difference to the health of the Orang Sungai, "With these tanks, the villagers need not rely on the river for drinking water, which is unhealthy because the river is used for bathing, washing and disposal of human waste. Many villagers had previously suffered from waterborne diseases such as cholera and typhoid."

BET and the Lodge raised RM12,080 (US$3,200) from local and international donors to purchase sixteen 400-gallon water tanks. These tanks would allow villagers to collect rainwater for drinking. Using its purchasing power, the Lodge was able to obtain the tanks for less money than if each villager had tried to purchase a water tank individually.

This project became important for staff morale as well as providing clean water for the community. Staff members were responsible for surveying villagers to determine which families did not have clean drinking water and that were most in need of a water tank. After much discussion, SRL selected 16 families from their list to receive a tank. The arrival of the tanks on August 17, 1998 was a time of great excitement for the village. People turned out in large numbers to watch the Minister of Tourism, Culture and Environment, YB Datuk Wilfred Bumburing officially give the tanks to the lucky families. Alison Culliford, author of <u>Paris Revisited</u> of the Orient Express Travel Series, was in attendance for the opening event and asked Albert how they would get the tanks home. Albert replied, "You will see. They are very resourceful. They will club together and get the ferry boat to deliver them." It turned out the recipients were too excited to wait for the ferry. The villagers had been so keen to get the tanks home they had loaded them onto their small boats, held on to the tank with one hand and blindly steered with the other. It made for a funny sight according to onlookers!

With such positive response from the community on the water tanks, the Lodge decided to undertake a second phase. In 1999, fundraising started again and by the next year, another RM30,400 (US$8,000) had been raised. This provided enough money to purchase water tanks for 38 families who did not have access to clean water.

Water tanks donated by various organisations includingf Rotary Club of KK South, Rotary Club of Tanjung Aru and tour companies

YB Datuk Wilfred Bumburing, Minister of Tourism with recipients of the water tanks in Sukau (1998)

A Rotarian presenting a water tank to a local villager (1999)

A housewife in front of her house with the water tank at right.

Albert Teo with members of Rotary Club of KK South checking out on the water tank

A house with a newly-installed water tank

The water tank project was helpful to many families, but it did not always work out as planned. On one of Albert's visits to Sukau, he went to see how the families were doing with the newly installed water tanks. He noticed that one of the water tanks had not been installed at one house. As this was the home of a man he knew well, Hamid, Albert asked him why he had not used the water tank. Albert recalls, "Hamid told me that they had encountered some unforeseen problems with their pigeons and the neighours' cats. Hamid's family had been keeping some pigeons in their house and these pigeons always hung around on the roof. The neighbours' cats often climbed up onto the roof to catch the pigeons. Both the pigeons and the cats had left droppings on the roof that made the rainwater undrinkable so it was not possible to use the water tank."

Official presentation of water tanks by Rotary Club of Tanjung Aru (1999)

Although there were some minor problems such as Hamid's, the water tank project became a benchmark in the Lodge's efforts to establish the benefits of ecotourism in Sukau. It made a direct improvement to the quality of life of the Orang Sungai and it was helpful in establishing good relations between the Lodge and the villagers. The manager during this time, Adrian Migiu, remembers, "When I came to Sukau in 1996, the feeling of animosity towards the Lodge was still strong among the people there. They didn't think that they got benefits from the Lodge. Then the turning point came when we did the water tank project in 1997. I had the opportunity to meet many of them in their own homes and explained to them what we were trying to do and that they would be benefiting from tourism. We also encouraged the locals to drop by the Lodge to let them see personally what we were doing. We showed them the slide show that we had for tourists and explained to them our purpose of building the Lodge there. Slowly their attitude to us started to change and they were quite happy when there were job openings for them and their children there.

Through the years, I became close to the locals. In turn, they benefited from the many projects we held in Sukau. The latest being the medical project which we helped organize. They were very appreciative of the effort that we made in the village."

Launching of the tree-planting project by Datuk Nahalan Hj. Damsal, Assistant Minister of Tourism (2000)

Tree-planting by members of UMS led by its Vice Chancellor Y. Bhg. Professor Datuk Seri Panglima Dr. Abu Hassan Othman & WWF Malaysia director (Sabah Operations), Dr. Geoffrey Davidson

Some members of the Korean medical team

Tree-planting by HRH Prince Henrik, Consort of Denmark together with WWF Malaysia chairman, Tengku Datuk Adlin (2002)

Group photograph with HRH Prince Henrik

Sukau Ecotourism Research & Development Centre

By 1999, Albert realized that many of the issues in the Kinabatangan region would need long term and complex solutions supported by environmental and social research. "It became more apparent that this was a new niche market which requires new solutions," he said. Sukau Ecotourism Research & Development Centre (SERDC) was created by Albert to meet this need. It would conduct research into local cultures, attitudes and the ecosystem.

SERDC emerged during a turbulent period in the Kinabatangan's development. There had been several cases of illegal logging. This activity, in addition to the government-approved clearing of the forest for large-scale oil palm plantations, meant wildlife habitat was quickly disappearing. Elephants were encroaching more frequently on palm plantations as a result. The increasing popularity of Sukau with tourists had resulted in overcrowding and overuse of some waterways, most notably, the Sungai Menanggul, a narrow tributary popular with wildlife watchers.

Elephant passing by the Lodge

Something needed to be done and quickly. Albert established SERDC to get involved at all levels in protecting the Kinabatangan's indigenous people and wildlife. The objectives as a result are diverse; from advocating for land protection; to community development projects; to research and testing of sustainable technology (see 'SERDC Objectives'). Funding for SERDC comes from Sukau Rainforest Lodge which contributes US$1 for every international tourist staying at the Lodge.

SERDC provided scholarships for guide training in 2001 when three Orang Sungai staff from Sukau Rainforest Lodge went to Kota Kinabalu to obtain their Green badges. The cost of this course including lodging, meals and course fee was RM6,167 (US$1,600). In May 2002, two more staff were sent to Kota Kinabalu for the guide training course.

Azizi Suhaimin with his brothers after his operation (2001)

SERDC has recently contributed to medical assistance projects. A local boy, Azizi Suhaimin B. Bahrani, was born with a cleft lip. In 2001, at four years of age, he was sent to the Duchess of Kent Hospital in Sandakan for the first of two operations. SERDC sponsored the lodging and food for his parents while they accompanied him to Sandakan. The second operation took place in February 2002. SERDC also provided a one year allowance of RM100 (US$26) per month for his three-year-old brother, Mohd Suhaizan, who suffers from the blood disease thalassaemia and requires monthly visits to Sandakan for blood transfusions. Support also came in a non-financial form when staff members of BET and Sukau Rainforest Lodge donated blood to the boy.

Signing of MOU between Albert Teo, Director of SERDC with Dr. Lin Ming Fung, Ph.D, President of Transworld Institute of Technology at the 2nd Taiwan Ecotourism Conference held 25-27 October 2004 at Douliu, Yunlin, Taiwan ROC.

Annemarie Rotzler of AESCH (white T-shirt) and agents with Roland Walker (2nd left), Palm Travel, Switzerland on educational tour of Sabah. Annemarie donated 1000SF to the tree-planting project of SERDC in Sukau (2004).

SERDC OBJECTIVES

Sukau Ecotourism Research & Development Centre or SERDC will assist :

1. To promote the gazetting of the proposed Kinabatangan Wildlife Sanctuary as soon as possible to prevent further loss of land to the plantations at the expense of wildlife by creating a greater awareness of its ecotourism potential through the local and international media.

2. To develop and apply the principles of ecotourism in the local community thus giving them alternative employment and income in addition to fishing, harvesting and hunting and ensuring the sustainability of the nature tourism industry in Sabah.

3. To provide students and teachers of ecotourism an avenue to learn about the concepts and practice of ecotourism as one possible solution to eradicating poverty in the rural community.

4. To test and apply modern technologies and environmental management practices in a local setting and to provide an economic model for sustainable development principles.

5. To act as a catalyst to develop a Code of Practice on ecotour operations and for lodge operations in Sukau.

6. To explore areas of co-operation and common interests among the various stakeholders in the Kinabatangan region including plantations, tourism lodges, tour operators, local community, and government departments including the Wildlife Department, Forestry Department, and Sabah Tourism together with the NGOs including Partners for Wetlands, WWF and University of Malaysia Sabah (UMS), to ensure the long term sustainability of ecotourism in Sabah.

SERDC provided sponsorship for a free medical clinic held in September 2003 for Sukau villagers. The clinic offered over 900 people treatments including general consultations, surgery, orthodontics, acupuncture, and dentistry. This project was carried out in collaboration with the Korean Medical Team, the Rotary Club of Kota Kinabalu South, and the Sukau Village Security and Development Committee. SERDC donated over RM10,780 (US$2,800) through free meals, transportation, accommodation, and airfare for the medical team and volunteers.

We chose Borneo Eco Tours/ Sukau Rainforest Lodge because of their eco friendly practices. When we came we were not disappointed.
Wong Hou Yuen, Subang Jaya, Selangor, Malaysia
22nd December 2000

The monkeys were great! I felt almost at home. The lodge is very cozy. I'm glad to be supporting an environmentally friendly business.
Daniel Sheehan, Deep Discoveries, Canada
8th February 2001

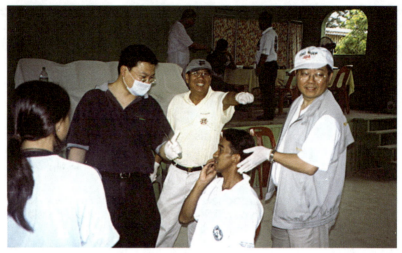

Tooth extraction in progress by Rotary Club of KK South

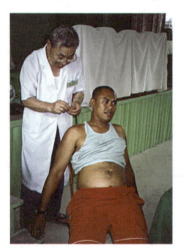

Saat receives Acupuncture treatment

A Rotarian doctor dispensing medicine

A group photograph of some Rotarians and Sukau villagers

The medical assistance provided at the clinic was very much appreciated by the locals. Dental treatment is one of the most needed services in this region and more than 200 people came to have decayed teeth extracted. One enthusiastic fellow returned three times to have teeth pulled. When the doctor spotted him for the fourth time in the line-up, he questioned why the villager had returned and warned him that it was dangerous to have too many teeth pulled in such a short time. The villager replied that he could only decide if there were still teeth hurting and needing extraction after he had one pulled! As he had many toothaches, he had to come back several times. Baton Bijamin also remembers on the last day Lodge staff getting their dental treatment under less than ideal conditions as the dentists had been overwhelmed with work during the clinic. "These extractions were done right on the jetty for three of the staff as all of the dentist's equipment had been stored in their vehicle the day before and the dentists needed to leave to catch their flight home," he said.

Sukau Tree Planting Project

SERDC and the Lodge decided to combat the deforestation of the Kinabatangan through a tree planting project. With many trees being lost to illegal logging and commercial agriculture in the Kinabatangan river basin, one of the aims of this project is to bring wide-spread attention to the problem, and to restore some of the forest habitat especially along the riverine reserve.

WWF Malaysia under their Partners for Wetlands Programme facilitated a reforestation program with the Sabah Forestry Department, Sabah Wildlife Department, Drainage and Irrigations Department, Land and Survey Department, the Rotary Club of Kota Kinabalu, and BET. The program was launched on June 4, 2000, to mark the World Environment Day occurring the next day, and was officiated by the Assistant Minister of Tourism Development, Environment, Science and Technology, Datuk Hj Nahalan Hj Damsal. As part of this initiative, BET and the Lodge 'adopted' 64 acres of riverine land at Tenegang that had been degraded by heavy logging and agricultural use. The plan was to reforest this land by planting small seedlings from native tree species. Tourists who stay at the Sukau Rainforest Lodge are given the opportunity to plant a tree on this site and if they wish, make a financial contribution to the program. Albert says, "It is also an opportunity to provide tourists staying at the Lodge a chance to participate in conservation, improve scenery during the river cruise, and enhance recognition of the Kinabatangan as an ecotourism destination. It also raises public awareness of the importance of sustainable development."

To maximize the economic benefits from this project, a villager was hired to collect the seedlings and a gardener was hired to tend the newly-planted trees. In the first year, 500 trees were planted; but they suffered a high mortality rate. Because the site had previously been used as a log dump the soil was very compacted. In this soil the seedlings struggled, and often failed, to grow roots. Elephants also trampled some of the young trees as they passed through the area.

Even with these disappointing losses, Albert still sees value from the project, "I'm not saying this tree planting project will change the world and save the global climate. But the act of planting the trees is educational for the villagers and my staff," he says, "It has helped to teach them the lesson that discipline and consistent hard work is the seed to long-term success, that caring for the community and the environment is part of the key to success for the Lodge; not just having good facilities and running a smooth operation."

This lesson was reinforced during a ceremonial visit by the President of WWF Denmark and His Highness the Consort of Denmark Prince Henrik in 2002. Prince Henrik came to Sukau Rainforest Lodge and participated in the tree planting project. The Prince was transferred by boat from the Lodge to the reforestation site and given his tree seedling to plant. All went well from a ceremonial perspective, but Albert was concerned that the tree would not survive. Albert recalls, "I was horrified to see that the site for the Prince's seedling had not been prepared adequately. The hole was five inches in diameter, barely large enough to accommodate the seedling. At the post-mortem briefing, it was my opportunity to explain that there was a need to have a larger hole however hard the ground might be. That just as in success, the more effort we put in to make a larger hole, the greater is the chance of not only survival; but also long term success;,that the greater the hole we dig for ourselves, the better our future will be."

"Biogas" Project

Some projects provided the chance to learn about cultural differences. One project that never quite achieved implementation was the "Biogas" project undertaken in 2001. In one of Albert's efforts to develop environmentally-friendly technology, he brought in experts from Thailand that would help them build a biogas treatment plant. This plant would convert human and animal wastes gathered in the village to free lighting and cooking gas.

Borneo Eco Tours sponsored site visits of the consultants and their meetings with the village committee made up of several representatives from the Sukau community. The village committee had been fully involved from the beginning and were very supportive of the project as it went through the preliminary design stages. Just prior to the project's official start, Albert and his managers decided to do one final check with the community and approached individual villagers of Muslim faith. "We wanted to determine if the project would have any religious implications," Albert said. This step avoided a potentially embarrassing outcome. After some conferring with religious leaders it was determined that the gas collected would be considered as "haram" and thus unclean for human use. Regrettably, the project was scrapped; but it reinforced the need for community involvement in all phases of project planning.

As a member of a family that has two generations dedicated to the US Forest Service, I fully appreciate the effort and conservation projects we've seen in the Sukau Rainforest. Great staff, a wonderful trip!
Valinda Mussa and Ibrahim Mussa, USA
20th February 2003

Such delightful, knowledgeable staff. Borneo Eco Tours has hired great people! I like your approach – supporting locals and being environmentally responsible; that's a large part of why I chose Borneo Eco Tours.
Sharon Delatlunt, Idaho, USA
5th January 2000

Terima Kasih banyak! It's very inspiring to come to an environmentally conscious tourist destination. If only all tourist operators shared the same ideals.
Alex Markham, Sydney, Australia
28th January 2000

Working With Partners

In addition to the worthwhile projects described in this chapter, SERDC has taken steps to extend its reach and make even greater contributions to a healthy Kinabatangan ecosystem. By partnering with other organizations such as government agencies, educational institutes and universities, SERDC is able to work on change at an institutional or structural level. These partnerships have been formalized through Memoranda of Understanding (MoUs) that outline the goals and responsibilities of the partners.

In 2000, SERDC signed a MoU with WWF Malaysia, and the University of Malaysia Sabah (UMS) to formulate an effective management plan for the conservation of the lower Kinabatangan river basin. This will also include work on ecotourism research and development in the area.

In 2001, SERDC signed another MoU with WWF Malaysia's Partners for Wetlands Programme to work on reforestation initiatives including the 64-acre adopted site mentioned earlier.

SERDC's work with WWF Malaysia and its Partners for Wetland Programme has been very important in establishing a regional vision for sustainable tourism development in the Kinabatangan river basin. The Sukau Rainforest Lodge has been held up as a working model of ecolodge development by the Partners for Wetland Programme. Other tour operators in the region have been encouraged to adopt some of its practices and philosophies and to engage in a discussion on how best to preserve the Kinabatangan. These initiatives will be discussed in the next chapter.

> This is an amazing place, friendly staff, knowledgeable guide; lots of wildlife not to mention the care and sensitivity towards a friendly Eco-environment. Truly a place and present worth visiting. I can't wait to come back and discover more.
> *Ken Tham, Toronto, Canada*
> 5th January 2002
>
> This was a most wonderful experience in a tranquil and friendly environment.....
> We hope it stays like this forever.
> *Nick and Karen Cowley, Hampshire, England*
> 19th June 2000
>
> We have had a great time with Joseph and the rest of the staff. Their kindness and hospitality is heart warming. We will recommend this special place to everyone back home especially because of the good environmental work they do. Thanks very much.
> *Van Noord and family, Nusa Ina, Holland*
> 26th July 2001
>
> I have been in Malaysia for almost 3 weeks now. Without a doubt you have the most courteous, helpful and considerate staff I've experienced. Your lodge is wonderful and the food is great. Thank you.
> *Bob Frishman, USA*
> 31st January 2003
>
> I enjoy being here, not only for your nice lodge, but also the wonderful wildlife experience I had here. Thank you for everything and wish to see you again.
> *Li Ning, China*
> 7th March 2003

Racquet-tailed Drongo

Chapter Ten

Changing the Tourism Industry:
Green Policies and Practices

"To cherish what remains of the Earth and to foster its renewal is our only legitimate hope of survival." Wendell Berry

The pressure on the Kinabatangan river basin is increasing. In addition to incidents of illegal logging and growing commercial agricultural operations, more tourists are coming to Sukau; and there are concerns that much of this tourism is not being developed in sustainable ways. Some reports show tourist visitation at Sukau has topped 2,000 people a month and sometimes as many as 25 boats crowd Sungai Menanggul, a narrow tributary of the Kinabatangan. This waterway has great wildlife viewing, but concern has been raised over its future. Nature guides say wildlife is stressed by the amount of boat traffic in the Sungai Menanggul and they worry the animals will move away or decline in numbers over time.

The WWF Malaysia's Partners for Wetlands Programme (PfW) held meetings with people using the Kinabatangan to determine their feelings and issues related to the River. They found that tour operators are not investing in the Kinabatangan for the long term because there is no tourism master plan for the area, and there is uncertainty over the legal status of the Kinabatangan Wildlife Sanctuary. The land was gazetted as a bird sanctuary under the Sabah Land Ordinance, but it still needs to be listed as a wildlife sanctuary under the Wildlife Conservation Enactment for it to be permanently protected.

The Partners for Wetlands are dealing with the lack of a tourism master plan by laying the groundwork for a community created tourism plan. PfW has been meeting with stakeholders from tourism, agriculture, logging, indigenous communities, and government sectors to determine their vision for the Kinabatangan river basin. Over many months they worked to gain consensus from the disparate interests on what the river would look like in the future. This process resulted in a vision of the floodplain in 2020 that will hopefully form the basis of a tourism master plan and guide overall development and conservation. The vision for tourism is shown in 'Ecotourism in 2020' *(next page)*.

The Lodge and Borneo Eco Tours have been very active participants in the Partners for Wetland project. They entered into a Memorandum of Understanding (MoU) with WWF's Partner for Wetlands Programme and the University of Malaysia Sabah with the intent of formulating an effective management plan for the Kinabatangan region. In 2001 BET entered into another MoU with WWF Malaysia, this time for a reforestation initiative.

Thank you for a wonderful ending to my holiday in Borneo. The lodge should be an inspiration and example to anyone hoping to provide such excellent facilities with so little impact on the surroundings. The lodge, the food, the service all excellent. All the staff have been so helpful and friendly and I would have seen so much less of the wonderful birds and animals without the eyes and ears of your dedicated guides.
Thank you.
Ian Foxall, Forest Trails, Great Britain
6th June 1996

As part of its efforts to develop a vision for a sustainable tourism industry, the Partners for Wetlands have promoted the adoption of a Code of Conduct or Practice among tourism operators. Codes of Practice setting out guiding principles and procedures have been used by many other industries to direct business conduct. By developing a Code of Practice for Sukau's tourism industry, PfW hopes that tourism operators will reduce negative impacts on the environment. Albert, Borneo Eco Tours and Sukau Rainforest Lodge have stepped forward in this arena and developed a Code of Practice (see 'Code of Practice') that hopefully will be adopted by other lodge owners.

This code conveys the underlying tenets of ecotourism at Sukau Rainforest Lodge and directs the Lodge's overall operation and the behaviours of visitors. It follows responsible tourism practices outlined by world tourism bodies such as the Pacific Asia Travel Association's Green Leaf program and the World Travel and Tourism Council (WTTC)'s Green Globe program; and covers conservation, education, environment and local community. Such items as "Be sensitive to the needs of the local people, fishermen and other tour operators when using the river" or "Trek on designated trails to minimise the damage to the habitat" provide direction for Lodge staff. Some of the code is aimed at guests; the item "Dress appropriately when visiting Sukau or the local homes" will help maintain good relations between the Lodge and the community and also make for a better visitor experience by reducing the chance of embarrassment or a culture clash.

SUKAU RAINFOREST LODGE

Code of Practice

Conservation

1. Strengthen the conservation effort of the places visited.

2. Support conservation programs and organizations working to preserve the environment.

3. Use natural resources efficiently e.g. water, energy.

Education

4. Educate the local community, guides, managers and tourists on the environment management policies of the company.

5. Educate guides, boatmen and tourists to never intentionally disturb wildlife habitats.

Environment

6. Limit the capacity of boats using Menanggul River to 8 persons. Larger boats are encouraged to operate only on the main Kinabatangan River.

7. Limit the maximum size of outboard engines to 15hp (preferably four stroke engines) when operating in Menanggul River to minimise noise and exhaust from engines. While viewing wildlife, show due consideration to both wildlife and other tourists in the other boats by using either electric motor or oar to manoeuvre your boat.

8. Practise recycling and proper disposal of waste products to minimise negative impact to environment.

9. Trek on designated trails to minimise damage to the habitat. Where appropriate, build raised plank-walks to minimize damage to trails with due consideration for existing elephant trails and trees.

Local Community

10. Be sensitive to the needs of the local people, fishermen and other tour operators when using the river.

11. Give priority to local people in employment opportunities whenever possible. Train and upgrade the skills of staff. For local community, provide contract jobs where appropriate or other forms of benefits including community and environment projects. Never give handouts and do charity in the long term but train them to be self-reliant and to deserve what they get.

12. Dress appropriately when visiting Sukau village or the local homes. Respect the sensitivities of local cultures.

13. Buy locally produced goods to benefit the local community but do not buy goods made from endangered species.

14. Where possible buy locally made boats to benefit the local people.

To help integrate ecotourism principles throughout the Lodge and BET, Albert has created a Green Productivity Team. Serving on the team are Baton Bijamin, General Manager/Director, BET; Susan Soong, Assistant General Manager, BET; Adrian Migiu, Manager/BET, Sandakan; Joseph Chong, Assistant Lodge Manager; Jamil, Supervisor, Sukau Rainforest Lodge; and Albert himself. These people meet regularly to discuss projects undertaken by SERDC and to monitor the use of environmental-friendly technologies at the Lodge. "We consistently review our practices and try to adopt new ecotourism principles and technologies for our operations," says Albert.

One of the other responsibilities of the Green Productivity Team was the creation of Green Policies for the Lodge that are shared with all guests (see 'Sukau Rainforest Lodge Green Policies'). These policies explain the unique features of the ecolodge, some of which they may notice during their stay, and helpful suggestions on how they can get the most out of their visit; for example, turning off their room fan when not in the room, or stopping the shower when shampooing.

SUKAU RAINFOREST LODGE
GREEN POLICIES

Thank you for choosing to stay at our "Green Lodge"!

We subscribe to the environmental codes of responsible tourism under Croon Globe program of World Travel and Tourism Council (WTTC) and PATA's Green Leaf program. To help you get the most out of your short stay at Sukau Rainforest Lodge, please read the information below.

1. **Electricity and Lighting**
A. Our Lodge does not have government electricity supply. Due to the high cost of solar technology, we use a hybrid system of generator and 20 units of solar photo-voltaic panels for our power requirement. Four units of GNB longlife dry-cell batteries and a 3KW Trace Pure Sinewave Power Inverter ensure a 24-hour uninterrupted supply of electricity and also allow you to enjoy the sound of the rainforest at night whilst minimising noise
    disturbance on wildlife.
B. At night lighting is supplemented by the use of kerosene oil lamps in the garden and along the corridors, recycled cooking oil lamps in the restaurant and lounge area to provide a cosy ambience.
C. Please switch off the lights and especially the ceiling fan when not in the room as the dry-cell batteries will discharge rapidly and may not last through the night.

2. **Water usage**
A. Our Lodge is also 100% self-sufficient on water. Rainwater is filtered for kitchen and guest use. This explains why we have many water storage tanks.
B. Hot water is supplied by 2 units of 132 gallons of Solarhart 300 JK solar heating systems.
C. Please help to conserve water especially to minimise flushing of toilets and turning off the taps when brushing, shampooing or soaping.

3. Disposal System

A. Our Lodge is equipped with proper septic tanks and nothing is discharged into the river. Organic materials are composted while non-biodegradable materials are separated and returned to Sandakan for disposal and recycling.

B. Please help us to dispose these into the bins labeled cans, bottles and plastic located at the open deck.

4. Noise

A. Much thought has gone into minimising noise level at the Lodge and on river cruises in order for guests to experience nature's symphony in the rainforest. This is why we adopt an open concept at the lounge area and restaurant. For this reason we do not encourage the use of television and radio.

B. Our generator has noise reduction acoustic insulation. This is used to charge our dry-cell batteries in the day time for overnight use.

C. Our boats are equipped with electric motors which are used when we move among wildlife sensitive areas to minimise noise and air pollution and to provide additional comfort to the passengers.

D. Please minimise noise level in your room after 9.00pm to avoid inconveniencing other guests.

5. Safety and Cleanliness

A. When you leave your room, drop the key at the pigeon hole provided next to the restaurant. Always lock up your valuables and cash or hand it to the Lodge Manager for safe-keeping as we will not be responsible for loss of valuables.

B. For your own safety, wear a life jacket at all times when on your river cruises.

C. Smoking and burning of candles or any materials are prohibited inside your room. Charging of commercial/TV batteries is also prohibited, as this will damage the power inverter. Fire extinguishers are located along the verandahs outside your rooms.

D. Do not eat foods, sweets and drinks in your room, as this will attract insects.

6. Design and Construction

A. The Lodge is built 100ft away from the river bank and outside the riverine reserve to prevent storm water soil erosion. Native vegetation is left intact to provide natural shading and to minimise impact of noise on the surrounding as well as to provide privacy to the resident guests.

B. The Lodge is built on stilts 5ft above ground to minimise impact of annual flooding of the Kinabatangan River and prevent ground insects, animals and reptiles from unwelcomed intrusion into the rooms.

C. An open concept is adopted for the lounge area and restaurant to allow for unimpeded air circulation and ventilation and thus minimise the use of fans.

D. The Lodge is built with local hardwood species including Belian (Borneo ironwood) for stilts and pillars, Merbau and Selangan Batu for open deck and balcony, Nyatoh for room furniture and fixtures, among others.

7. Local Community Participation

A. Where possible we try to provide employment opportunities for the local community. The wooden boats, jetty, plank walks, open deck, wall paneling, wooden benches and deck tables/chairs are all testimony of their capabilities.

B. 80% of our staff are locals. As most of the local staff could not speak English when they joined us we have instituted training and brought overseas tourism students to help them understand the cultures and needs of the tourists, to develop communication skill and speak English. We hope we have trained them to run the Lodge to your expectation and also maximised their natural ability as guides for the river cruises and jungle walks.

C. Your patience and encouragement for any shortcomings will go a long way in helping them to overcome language and cultural barriers.

THANK YOU FOR YOUR KIND CO-OPERATION!

ALBERT C.K.TEO
MANAGING DIRECTOR
BORNEO ECO TOURS / SUKAU RAINFOREST LODGE

Rarely do you find a lodge both ecologically sensitive and able to meet the guests' need of comfort, care and activity. Sukau Rainforest Lodge is a shining star in the ecotourism world. The guides (Joey is terrific!), boatmen, service staff, Leonard, Joseph and that fantastic chef, were so attentive and friendly that the Lodge felt like home very quickly. From the tree planting to the Orang-utan plus Proboscis spotting to the bird watching, our adventures are marvellous. The scenic beauty and serenity of Sukau are memorable. Thank you for your hospitality and thank you for your commitment to preserving our environment for future generations.
Richard C. Bell, Journey Travel, New York City, USA
18th March 2001

Enforcement

As WWF Malaysia discovered in the Partners for Wetland project, tourism operators are not always making choices when building or running their lodges with the long-term health of the environment in mind; at times it appears that the pressure to make profits are the main driving force. Part of this problem stems from valid concerns over the area's future. Businesses will not invest their money into a nature-based tourism region if the habitats are not being protected and land tenure is not secure. With the real possibility of losing the natural attractions that tourism businesses need to operate in, there will be a tendency to make money quickly with little thought to community development or conservation. PfW is trying to overcome this issue with their multi-year vision of the Kinabatangan and encouragement of long-term investment.

At times, it is a daunting challenge. There have been flagrant violations of Sabah's environmental regulations in the past. In 1999, there were two cases of illegal logging that caused major destruction along the river; one site was only 20 minutes upriver by boat from the government's Forestry office causing people to wonder why it was not stopped. This logging caused great concern among local people and tourism businesses who saw this activity as a major threat to their survival. "The Orang Sungai are very unhappy that the future of the tourism industry in Sukau is numbered while outsiders are benefiting from the illegal logging," Albert said at the time. "The illegal loggers are once again putting the future of wildlife in Sukau in danger for greed of money and short term gain."

Tourism operators were united and loud in their criticism of the illegal logging and efforts have been made to stop it. Now the tourism operators are under scrutiny themselves as the number of boats and visitors threaten the quality of wildlife watching and possibly disturb sensitive environments. In response to increasing tourism levels at Sukau, a Wildlife Department centre is being constructed near the junction of the Sungai Menanggul and the Kinabatangan River. A gate will also be placed at this entrance of the Sungai Menanggul to restrict the number of boats using the waterway at any one time. There will be rules regarding boat size, and engine and passenger numbers in the future. While this will hopefully reduce some of the problems arising from crowding, some people have expressed concerns that it will only add to the bureaucracy without making any long-term contribution to habitat health.

> Very good resort. Should be congratulated in pioneering ecotourism in this region and proving there is an alternative economic activity to logging and palm oil. Keep it up.
> *Phillip Clarkson, San Michelle, Sydney, Australia*
> 18th October 1998
>
> One of the most beautiful places of the world, the people are very kind and we hope this beauty will be conserved for Mankind.
> *Dr. Andan Odu, Zoological Garden, via Windrose, Berlin*
> 21st February 1999

Industry Recognition and Awards

Sukau Rainforest Lodge and Borneo Eco Tours have been recognized by the tourism industry for their leadership in creating a world-class ecotourism product. Their innovative approach to blending community development, conservation and tourism have netted them many prestigious awards. The awards range from Sabah's Tourism Gold awards to the highly-sought British Airways Tourism For Tomorrow honour (see 'Albert Teo's Award Winning Businesses'). Three times BET received the annual World Tourism and Travel Council's Green Globe Achievement Award, a sign Albert's efforts had been recognized amongst tourism's largest organizations.

Albert Teo's Award Winning Businesses	
Sukau Rainforest Lodge	
International Hotel and Restaurant Association Environment Award (1999)	Runner-up
International Hotel and Restaurant Association Green Hotelier of the Year (1999)	Runner-up
Sabah Tourism Gold Award (1999/2000)	Excellence in Hotel Services (2-Star and Lodges)
Borneo Eco Tours	
Sabah Tourism Gold Award (1990)	Best Tourism Publication
Sabah Tourism Gold Award (1990)	Best Photograph
Malaysian Tourism Gold Award (1990)	Best Tour Package – 1st Runner-up
Malaysian Tourism Gold Award (1990)	Best Publication – 1st Runner-up
Malaysian Tourism Gold Award (1992)	Best Incentive Package – Merit
European Incentive and Business Travel Meetings (EIBTM) Award (1994)	Most Visionary Green Incentive Concepts
World Travel and Tourism Council (WTTC) Green Globe 21 (1996, 1998, 2000)	Achievement Award
Sabah Tourism Award (1997)	Best Inbound Tour Operator
British Airways Tourism for Tomorrow Award (1997)	Best Ecolodge Pacific Region - winner
Malaysian Tourism Gold Award (1997)	Best Tour Operator – Merit
Malaysian Tourism Gold Award (1997)	Best Tour Package – Merit
Malaysian Tourism Gold Award (2003)	Best Tour Program – Merit
Travelasia Breakthrough Eco-Awards (1999)	Best Tour Operator
Sabah Tourism Gold Award (1999/2000)	Best Tour Operator
Conde Nast Traveler Ecotourism Award (1999)	Tour Operator – Honourable Mention

For Albert, the awards are a validation that he has exceeded environmental standards and created a product that meets tourism expectations in a competitive and quickly-changing world. "I have on my side a unique product," Albert says, "The awards prove it."

Albert also thinks the awards his organization has garnered will lead to positive change at a regional level within Malaysia as ecotourism spreads and spin-offs to local communities multiply. He sums it up by saying, "I hope the awards will bring about greater development in our ecotourism industry which will eventually benefit both the local communities in the rural and remote areas of Sabah and the environment. Ecotourism is about sustainable management of the natural resources that we have."

A night is not enough. I enjoyed a lot. I won't forget. Thank you.
Gil (Jong) Sung, Korea
3rd June 2003

What a wonderful experience! You have created a place where people can enjoy the beauty of wildlife without spoiling it. You truly deserve to call yourselves Borneo Eco Tours. The beautiful lodge and friendly staff were an added bonus. Thank you all very much!
Carlo & Marilene vd Brznd, Netherlands
24th July 2003

We are having a fantastic honeymoon in Malaysia and to date SRL has been the highlight of the holiday. We have seen creatures in their natural habitat that we have only seen on television at home. We had a great time thanks to the staff and our guide John, who are all very friendly, genuine people. Hope Eco-tourism in Malaysia booms!
Alan/Maire McDevitt, Ireland
7th October 2003

Let me show my gratitude for the kindness of all staffs here. Jungle cruises are excellent, but nothing is so impressive as the hospitality of handsome boys and cute girls here. Although my staying here was so short I refreshed myself during the stay. Hoping for coming back here again before long. Thankyou so much.
Masaki Yoneyama, Japan
3rd November 2003

"I am presently planning my 18th visit to the Sukau Rainforest Lodge. There are so many reasons. The staff at the lodge as well as local village people are friendly and welcoming; the foggy mornings when one can scarcely see in front of the boat on the river and then suddenly the fog clears and the rainforest and other vegetation along the river suddenly becomes alive with birds as they dry their wings and start to forage; the times when it rains and rains and rains until the rivers spread out over their banks for distances as far as you can see; the tranquility of sitting in a small boat and either just floating along with the tides and currents or using a quiet electric motor and watching the wildlife surrounding you....... I could continue.... The beauty of birds the colour of bright jewels that flit through the jungles and elephant grass, the fascination of watching the long fur on a large male orang utan blow in the breeze as he lay in his leafy bower in the late afternoon, a pygmy elephant herd in the edge of the jungle who were all flapping their ears so hard on a hot afternoon that you could hear the ears flapping before you saw the herd, the pygmy elephant herd crossing the river, the sound of the hornbills' wings moving through the air as they fly overhead, the beautiful butterflies, the flying lizards...... The total vertebrate species list for the Sukau area has now passed the 350 mark.... And many species groups have been almost neglected in this total. Where else in this modern noisy rushing world can one withdraw to a place where there is no TV; where staff and guests alike stop their activities to see the otter family swim by in front of the lodge or the elephants investigate the plankway in the rainforest behind the lodge.... And all of this comes with hot water in the showers! I can understand why Albert Teo refers to the place with words such as "paradise".....
Dale Straughan
17 October 2004

Looking To The Future

"I have always stated it is ten times easier to build an ecolodge than it is to maintain it once it is open," Albert Teo says. This observation can be sobering when one remembers the many challenges there were in securing the Lodge's building site, wrestling financing from banks, and setting up a construction site in the middle of a jungle. Those problems were just the beginning. Albert and his staff at Sukau Rainforest Lodge have dealt with floods, cash flow shortages, downturns in the tourism industry, illegal logging, and resentment from villagers. Any of these events could have spelled the end of the Lodge, but under Albert's leadership, and with a bit of good fortune, Sukau Rainforest Lodge overcame them. It not only continues to exist, but has ambitious plans for the future. As discussed in earlier chapters, new facilities such as the games room and individual cabins will open in 2006 and marketing activities are targeting new customer groups in Asian countries to increase visitation.

Thanks so much for making us feel at home and in awe with the magnificent surroundings. Staff were just wonderful, helpful and full of humour. Personally I would like to say: This (Sukau) is your home. It is the very best place in the world. (Don't let anybody tell you otherwise!!) Keep it the way it is because our kids need to know this too. You see, we did not inherit this magnificent world from our forefathers; we borrowed it from our kids. Absolutely magical!
Rudd Kleinpaste, Project Expeditions, Auckland, New Zealand
12th March 2001

Lessons Learned

Albert and his team learned several lessons since the Lodge opened its doors in 1995. They range from the global to the minuscule, but provide useful information for anyone contemplating the plunge into the ecotourism industry. Albert recalls his biggest challenge was "coping with fallout of the post-1997 financial challenge where we were short of cash flow to repay the bank loan, and needed to handle staff and community suspicions all at the same time;" but there have been many other obstacles that have clarified for him the elements that must be in place for a lodge to succeed. These lessons are summed up in the following sections.

1. Ecolodges Need Protected Spaces To Survive

Ecolodges need a healthy wilderness as a setting for tours and adventure activities. Formal protection of habitat in the form of parks or wildlife sanctuary, as seen at the Kinabatangan Wildlife Sanctuary, is critical for longterm success. Where protected areas exist, government must enforce its own regulations so that illegal land use or poaching does not occur.

The tourism industry can also work with government where tourism activities are contributing to the negative pressures on the environment. Codes of Practices can encourage long-term sustainability in the tourism industry by modifying lodge or tour activities and operating practices. "Sustainability of wildlife will be a major concern as the number of tourists increase and as other operators use boats and engines with bigger capacity that will affect the quality of ecotourism experiences," Albert says of the lower Kinabatangan river basin. By adopting a Code of Practice for Sukau Rainforest Lodge, he is encouraging ecotourism practices in the Kinabatangan river basin, such as taking smaller tour sizes.

Non-profit or non-governmental organizations can be important partners in working to save the protected areas ecolodges need. These organizations may be viewed as neutral parties by non-tourism businesses or government, allowing for open discussions among stakeholders. Their neutral status can help broker solutions to environmental problems and preserve sensitive habitats. WWF Malaysia has been an important ally for the Lodge in trying to protect the Kinabatangan floodplain through the WWF Partners for Wetlands project (for more information, see Chapter One). Most ecolodges would benefit from similar partnerships.

2. Governments Can Help Ecotourism Through Tax Incentives

The Lodge finds it challenging to maintain financial profitability because of its unique nature and location. Governments can help ecolodges and other ecotourism businesses in these situations by offering greater tax incentives than offered at present. Tax incentives for businesses willing to locate in rural areas would help offset some of the increased transportation costs found when operating in remote areas like the lower Kinabatangan. Increased tax incentives or training grants could also be used to encourage more employment of locals and more investment in ecotourism skills training.

Regulations on land ownership and taxation would also benefit from a review. "At present, a company does not qualify for tax incentives unless it is 60 per cent owned by Bumiputeras (indigenous population), but the majority of rural communities who will benefit from such projects are Bumiputeras," he says. This policy will only serve to limit investment and special loans to investors who cannot qualify under this condition.

3. Financial Institutions Need Special Guidelines For Ecolodges

Ecolodges need support from financial institutions and Albert found that getting this support was one of his most daunting challenges in building the Lodge. It is highly unlikely that ecolodge owners will have sufficient funds to build a lodge without borrowing and obtaining financing terms that can be met from seasonal operations is a major challenge. Ideally, ecolodges could benefit from bank or government loans with lower interest rates, and repayment terms of ten to 15 years that would recognize the longer gestation time of ecotourism projects. As he described in earlier chapters, financial institutions can have very stringent collateral requirements when ecolodges are located in remote sites. Relaxing these requirements would free up capital for investing in an ecolodge and allow some people to purchase or build an ecolodge even if they may not have significant assets to meet existing bank security guidelines.

4. Tourists Are Not Familiar With Ecotourism Or Willing To Pay A Premium For An Ecotour

The concept of ecotourism is still unknown among mass tourists and it appears that marketing of green products is losing steam in a world more preoccupied with global security. Part of the problem may have arisen in the past as tour operators used the term 'ecotourism' with abandon, labelling everything from a gift shop with a view of nature to a white-water rafting experience as an ecotour.

"Unfortunately the term 'ecotourism' has been misused and it may be difficult to get the true meaning across to mass travelers and have a bigger impact," Albert says. Conveying the philosophy behind ecotourism and the premium price it deserves for its authentic, small-scale experience with no economies of scale is difficult. "The 'enlightened travelers' of the future who will continue to seek out and pay for this spiritual experience that ecotourism can provide, will still be a minority," Albert states. But ecolodge operators must succeed in distinguishing their product if they are to achieve financial success. Albert predicts, "Unless the lodge is one of a kind in the area and is able to charge a premium price, it is unlikely there is going to be the financial resources that will allow the lodge to undertake the elaborate or international marketing needed to make it profitable."

Certification programs such as the Green Globe or Green Leaf awards have helped somewhat in identifying and verifying ecolodge quality, but many of these awards are not well recognized by the traveling public, and holding these awards has not translated to higher tour prices for operators. Too often the burden of distinguishing their lodges and the justification for a premium price is tackled by individual lodge owners in their marketing plans, which leads to the next lesson.

5. Market Aggressively

As has been demonstrated time and again, ecolodge owners must understand marketing and employ a variety of marketing techniques to survive. "Do cooperative marketing with other lodges, work with ecotourism wholesalers, host travel writers, build a good website, and look for opportunities wherever you can find them," Albert suggests. "Attend trade shows or join forces with those who can afford to attend." Without strong marketing, ecolodges will not be able to compete with other tourist lodges that often cut prices to sell tours. He cautions against getting caught up in a price war as it can seriously harm an ecolodge's long term potential, "Competition based on price will further degrade tour quality making it more difficult to keep prices realistic and maintain the quality of a unique ecotourism and wildlife tourism product."

6. Lodge Owners Need Strong Character And Business Backgrounds

Anyone contemplating a business as an ecolodge owner must look carefully in the mirror. That person will need a special combination of character and business skill and acumen. Albert suggests that an ecolodge owner will need to function well in each of the following areas and offers his suggestions for success:

- Design – Determine what you want in a lodge.
- Construction – Be honest in how much you can afford to spend. Figure out the best way to build on your site.
- Negotiation – Secure ownership of the building site to provide long term security and collateral to financial institutions.

- Operations – Start by determining what standard of service you are aiming for; the rest will follow from there.
- Ecotourism – Read up on the topic and attend seminars or conferences to stay on top of trends and issues.
- Marketing – Attend trade shows or find others to partner with.
- Tour packaging and tour operations – Learn photography to save money; use the Internet and a good website to market your ecolodge.
- Manpower training and development – Train leaders to train the local people; provide field trips for staff exposure; teach staff to develop personal development skills such as regular savings and reading habits.
- Continuous improvement – Learn to solicit guest feedback; use guest comments to plan new facilities.
- Community relations – Plan informal meetings or meals with local community leaders to build rapport and minimise suspicions. Ask these leaders what they need and what they want to see happen in the community.

An ecolodge owner will need to have passion and be willing to work long and hard. As Albert has found, it will take perseverance and a good support team who share your vision to succeed. Having money to invest in the project and the funds to support yourself until an ecolodge achieves breakeven is also important for lodge owners. And above all, you must understand the ecotourism industry. "Don't build an ecolodge unless you have worked in one to gain experience so as to minimize mistakes which can be very costly, and to be sure that this is really what you want to do," he cautions. "Many timber millionaires have learnt a bitter lesson in this area. After finding that there is no more money to be made in timber, these business owners ventured into ecotourism and tried to make big money without proper study or research. They ended up building a 'white elephant'; ecotourism facilities or lodges that destroyed the very environment that they needed to protect and promote. Often these millionaires closed their 'ecotourism' businesses down after a few years, losing a lot of money in the process. A better way to enter the ecotourism industry is to go overseas and visit other ecolodges, read books, research what you want first, know the terrain and the unique selling propositions of the area. Engage an experienced person in the field of ecotourism. Pay a bit more up front to save a lot more in perpetuity."

7. Motivating Staff Requires Creativity And Leadership

The right staff will make day-to-day operations much more efficient, and the right people will be an important marketing tool as they can execute your vision for customer service. This is difficult in remote locations where finding and retaining staff requires additional training, and convincing locals of the desirability of working in ecotourism. The Lodge has worked hard to recruit and train the people needed to make Sukau a success and believes that achieving success in this area is critical for an ecolodge. Staff morale can waiver under the stress of running an ecolodge and requires regular bolstering to keep staff motivated. As one of the early managers, Benjamin Denis, recalls, "Today I think working at the Lodge was one of the greatest challenges in my career." He feels the most important lesson he learned in the area of staff motivation was the need for continuous reinforcement of the actions he wanted to see. "Regular pep talks, fortnightly training sessions, reading programs and cash incentives are very important," Albert says and all have been used successfully at the Lodge to keep people learning and performing their jobs to a high level.

8. Community Projects Are Critical To An Ecolodge's Success

Sukau Rainforest Lodge has been active in the community from its first year of operations. The programs it has undertaken from the water tanks, to the weed control, to the medical clinics have built bridges with the local people and provided direct benefits from the Lodge to the community. "These community projects have been critical in building goodwill with the Lodge neighbours," Albert says. He did learn from some of the projects that even where you try to do good work, problems can arise. The first water tank project had an unexpected negative side effect when jealousy was created between those families who received water tanks and those who did not. Since then, he has learned, "There is a need to involve the community leaders in these projects as much as possible. You need to let them decide what they need and figure out how to spread the benefits around as much as possible. We are now focusing more on what they deserve and less on what they need so that we don't perpetuate a dependency syndrome." By constantly looking for ways to participate and contribute to the community in which an ecolodge is located, many of ecotourism's benefits can be realized.

> We hope you will succeed in maintaining the Eco-tourism for many years to come..........
> *Danish FAM Trip/Billetkonteret*
> 29th May 2000
>
> How can we let the world know about this beautiful place and still allow it to keep its innocence?
> *Leonie Spaccavento, Australia*
> 23rd September 2000

The Future

Even with the Lodge's success, Albert is not slowing down. He is making plans for new sustainable tourism initiatives. He is hoping to use what he has learned from Sukau Rainforest Lodge to build a water-based ecolodge along the coastline in Sabah. Asians have always enjoyed a close relationship with water and often choose to live on it or near it. Despite this, they sometimes abuse this relationship by using the water as a convenient place for waste disposal. He hopes to build a new lodge that will use sustainable technology similar to that seen at Sukau Rainforest Lodge, but will also provide a model for local residential communities. The technology used at this water-based lodge will dispose of wastes in environmentally-friendly ways and will also be inexpensive and easy to install and operate. This will allow villagers to see technology up-close that can be adapted to their homes. By making the new lodge a living demonstration project, it is hoped that he can influence people living on the water to adapt the technology his lodge uses.

> We were very impressed with the Lodge being a true "Ecological" lodge. The impact on the land has been minimal. We very much enjoyed the river cruises and were fortunate to see many birds, monkeys and monitor lizards. The staff was friendly, attentive and seemed to enjoy their jobs. Our guide was excellent. He is very knowledgeable of the flora and fauna of this area. We will always remember our time spent here. Thank you.
> *Jim and Kim Dorvee, Asia Transpacific Journeys, Boulder, USA*
> 22nd October 1997

It is obvious that Albert Teo has been the driving force behind the creation of the Lodge and the community projects it has undertaken, but he is making sure other people can steer the Lodge into the future. He has selected talented people and nurtured them through ongoing professional and personal development programs to take on ever greater responsibilities at the Lodge. He believes that the more successful the Lodge and the greater the overall knowledge and experience of his staff, the less vulnerable the Lodge is to problems when he eventually retires. "Ironically, the more successful Sukau Rainforest Lodge is, the more likely it will continue to go on after I leave the scene. Therefore it must become better with the years," Albert says.

Albert sees the need to create a body of knowledge that will preserve the Lodge's legacy and help with the transfer of information from one generation of staff to the next. The books he has written are an important part of this strategy. "I believe it is necessary to record the Lodge's early history and struggles and the people who made it happen so that a legacy is created for future generations and staff," Albert says. "People will come and go, but the body of knowledge will remain to ensure continuity."

When looking back on the Lodge's first decade of operations and reflecting on his most important contribution in reaching its current level of success, Albert is extremely modest. He does not point to any one action or management strategy, but instead focuses on the efforts he made to live up to one man's faith in him. "It is not what I did, but more so my response to the vision of Kari (the original landowner). The fact that the company was able to buy the land and be assured of the long term security of our investment, and Kari's faith in us, gave me the commitment to persevere in the face of the early losses and numerous challenges. I could not let people down. I am willing to invest further in the Lodge in lieu of other locations to generate greater benefits and more jobs for them."

It appears that Kari's faith was not misplaced. As Kari remembers, he was severely criticised by his neighbours for selling his land to the Lodge. The villagers berated him and questioned his judgement, but Kari knew that the land was of little use if left idle and he felt he could create a better future for his family if he let the land be used for the ecolodge. With Albert's careful stewardship and innovative management, Kari has been proven right. "With the money I got from selling off the land, I was able to pay for the schooling of my two children, buy a generator and a 15hp outboard engine, purchase a van for transport, and pay for my daughter's wedding. I also feel happy for the Lodge being there because I can earn a little bit of return from the Lodge as they provide me with extra income as a part-time boatman when the need arises. If I don't have any assignments from them, still I am happy as I can just go out to the river and cast my nets to catch fish and prawns. I can sell it to survive another day. I am particularly happy to see that the Lodge is engaging locals from this area, apart from my children, to work in the Lodge. The Lodge is benefiting the locals so it shows I did not make the wrong decision when I sold the land to the company."

The villagers have also seen an improvement in their lives with the success of the Lodge. The community projects undertaken by the Lodge and SERDC have presented learning experiences for the staff at times, but they have delivered positive changes to the community. Awang, one of Kari's sons-in-law, says, "With Sukau Rainforest Lodge in Sukau, it has given the opportunity to the local kids to work and earn some income; provide water tanks to the locals; obtain free medicals; and it gives the village homeowners the opportunity to operate as a guesthouse or home stay when there are tourists in the area. I am thankful to the kindness of Mr. Albert Teo and his contributions to the village which have benefited a lot of people."

Equally as important as the community contributions, the Lodge has attracted the attention of tourists around the world. For those people looking for intimate adventures with nature and Sabah's wildlife while being assured they will step gently on the earth, Sukau has it all. But the best environmental-friendly technology in the world cannot satisfy a traveler's need to connect with the rare and unusual in our world. Sukau Rainforest Lodge succeeds because it puts people in a remarkable setting, and then surrounds them with the warmth and friendliness of its staff and the community. The Lodge and BET's desire to be good stewards, and its generosity in sharing its success and resources with the community and conservation organizations, can be felt in every aspect of the Lodge's activities. Guests may not always understand ecotourism but they understand that Sukau Rainforest Lodge is unique. They enjoy a great holiday and they reconnect with the natural world. And that is the real legacy of Sukau Rainforest Lodge.

> *"In the end, our society will be defined not only by what we create, but by what we refuse to destroy."* – The Nature Conservancy's John Sawhill

Epilogue

The success of Sukau Rainforest Lodge has been the fulfillment of my own dream to move from personal success in the first half of my life to one of significance in the latter part of my life.

I have experienced first-hand the generosity of the community especially from Kari, as they have worked with me to build a viable ecotourism business that would not only give people an opportunity to enjoy an out-of-the-way wildlife experience, but also create economic and cultural and social benefits in the region and preserve precious environments.

The *Orang Sungai* connection to the land and their commitment to their community have reinforced my decision to invest in ecotourism. I will continue to make Sukau Rainforest Lodge a priority in my business and where necessary will divert resources to this project so that I can help the villagers in Sukau enjoy a better quality of life.

Albert Teo

Albert Teo

Albert Teo is a prominent figure in Borneo's tourism industry. His expertise as an hotelier and a tour operator is reflected in the success of his companies, Borneo Eco Tours, Sukau Rainforest Lodge and Borneo Backpackers, and in the number of directorships he holds for several large hotel properties. Albert's dedication to customer service, community partnerships and environmental stewardship, have earned him many loyal customers and the esteem of the travel industry. His businesses have received many professional accolades, including the prestigious British Airways Tourism for Tomorrow award in 1999 (Best Ecolodge / Pacific region), the World Travel and Tourism Council's Green Globe Achievement awards in 1996, 1998 and 2000, and the Malaysian Tourism Gold Award (Best Tour Operator/Merit) in 2003.

Albert is a keen nature photographer, capturing new images as he explores the cultures and wild spaces of Malaysia. His images grace over 150 postcards and bookmarks on Sabah, Brunei, and Sarawak. He has also published six photographic guide books on Borneo, including **Sabah: Land of the Sacred Mountain** and **Journey Through Borneo**. Albert is also a keen jungle trekker; to-date he has covered over 1,000 kilometers in the wilds of Borneo.

Albert is a Fellow of the Hotel Catering and International Management Association (FHCIMA) in the United Kingdom, a Certified Hotel Administrator (CHA) in the USA, and hold's Sabah's professional MOCAT tourist guide certification. He was Chairman of the Malaysian Association of Tours and Travel Agents or MATTA Sabah Chapter In 1991/92 and from 1996 to 2001. He served on The International Ecotourism Society's board of advisors from 1996 to 2004, and on the Sabah Environment Protection Association from 1996 to 2000. Albert is a current member of the Sabah Tourism Board marketing committee.

Carol Patterson

Carol Patterson is a well-known ecotourism industry consultant, lecturer, author and seminar leader. She heads Kalahari Management Inc., a consulting firm based in Calgary, Canada, that provides feasibility studies, business planning, and training for the nature based tourism industry. She is the author of a quarterly newsletter **EcoTourism Management** which furnishes information on the ecotourism industry and related business items and practices and is the author of two books. **The Business of Ecotourism** offers business guidance for individuals, companies and organizations involved in the nature tourism industry; and **The Business of Ecotourism** – *Teacher's Edition* for teachers of ecotourism concepts. She is also a co-author of a book on ecotourism business planning used by The Nature Conservancy in their tourism projects in Latin America.

Carol has degrees in Business Administration, Economics and Geography, and holds a Certified Management Accountant designation. In 1991 she was named Merit Winner in the Pannell Kerr Forster Research Award competition.

Carol is an active member of various community organizations. She is a private pilot, and created and operated the "Flying Zoo to You" program for the Calgary Zoo from 1985 to 1987. A Senator of the Calgary Zoological Society, Carol has contributed to the live collections, education and business operations committees and is a Past President of the Society. She also serves on the board of Watchable Wildlife Inc, a U.S. non-profit organization promoting responsible wildlife viewing practices and ethics.

If you would like to contact Carol, email her at carol@kalahari-online.com or call 01-403-290-0805. Information on her books, newsletter and research studies can be found at http://www.kalahari-online.com.

When I (Albert) started working in the tourism industry, I could not have envisioned the path my life would take. From my earliest days as a student of economics at the University of London, I was interested in business and the travel industry but only after much persuasion from my late father. I followed a somewhat predictable path by working in the family hotel in Kota Kinabalu and later set up its subsidiary tour company. But through my travels in Sabah and Sarawak, I became more and more enamoured with the wildlife that is so unique to Malaysia. I wanted to develop a type of travel that contributed to conservation, help generate employment opportunity and uplift the living standard at the local level, while providing a relaxing holiday. Some people were calling this type of travel "ecotourism", and the more I read, the more I knew this was a philosophy I wanted to incorporate into my business activities. By the early 1990s, I had decided to commit my time and money to building Sukau Rainforest Lodge, and the adventure of a lifetime began.

There have been challenges I could not have anticipated and at times, the goals I had set for myself seemed daunting. When the outlook seemed bleak, I was bolstered by the support of people in many different fields, and humbled by their faith in my abilities. Their help has meant that there is a Lodge ten years later to write about.

It is important to thank those people, and others, for their contributions. Without them, the two aspects of this project - the building of the Lodge and the completion of this book - would not have been possible. Firstly, appreciation must be given to the Sukau villagers who allowed the Lodge to be built in their community and then passed along their recollections of the early years for the book, particularly Kari bin Ongong and his son-in-law, Awang. We would also like to recognize the efforts of the government officials including Encik Latiff Kandok, Kota Kinabatangan District Officer; Dr. Robert Ong, Forestry Department; Mahedi Andau, Director, Wildlife Department; all of whom helped over the years to deal with the regulations and permits needed to make the Lodge a reality.

A big "Thank You" must also be extended to YB Tan Sri Datuk Chong Kah Kiat, Deputy Chief Minister cum Minister of Tourism, Culture and Environment for his continuous encouragement and for writing the book's foreword, and also toYg. Bhg Datuk Monica Chia, Permanent Secretary, Ministry of Tourism, Culture and Environment for her personal interest in our project. Also to all of our friends and partners overseas who have been supporting our community, medical and environment projects. Our heartfelt thanks for making a difference in Sukau and the lower Kinabatangan basin. The World Wildlife Fund, particularly Y. M. Tengku Datuk Dr. Zainal Adlin Bin Tengku Mahmood, Chairman, WWF Malaysia; Dr Geoffrey Davison, Director, Borneo Program, WWF Malaysia; and Datuk Rajah Indran, Project Manager, Partners for Wetlands Programme who are working with BET and the Lodge to save the Kinabatangan and the precious wildlife found there. And to Y. Bhg Professor Datuk Seri Panglima Dr. Aby Hassan Othman, Vice-Chancellor, University of Malaysia Sabah for his encouragement. Your leadership in this region has been invaluable and has done much to bring disparate groups together in a discussion of the Kinabatangan's future.

We would also like to thank the former and present staff of Borneo Eco Tours and Sukau Rainforest Lodge for taking the time to tell their stories of living and working at the Lodge, as well as working tirelessly to make the Lodge a success from its early years to the present. Thank you as well to Duncan Butchart for his beautiful watercolour illustrations of birds of the Kinabatangan river, Hitesh Mehta for his invaluable comments and Don Morberg for lending his editing and communication expertise; their patience is greatly appreciated. And our acknowledgements would not be complete without recognising the support of our families, who have cheered us on through the difficult times and allowed us the time to put this book together.

Albert Teo & Carol Patterson

Further Readings

1. The Kinabatangan Floodplain by WWF Malaysia.

2. A Field Guide to the Mammals of Borneo by Payne, Francis and Phillipps

3. Pocket Guide to the Birds of Borneo by Sabah Society.

4. The Natural History of Orang Utan by Elizabeth L. Bennett

5. Issues and Challenges in Developing Nature Tourism in Sabah by IDS

6. Proceedings of 1999 World Ecotourism Conference: The Right Approach by IDS

7. Ecotourism: A Guide for Planners and Managers by the International Ecotourism Society Volume 1 & 2

8. Ecotourism: Principles, Practices and Policies for Sustainability by Megan Epler Wood

9. Tourism, Ecotourism and Protected Areas by Hector Ceballos-Lascurain

10. The Ecolodge Sourcebook for Planners and Developers by The International Ecotourism Society

11. International Ecolodge Guidelines by Hitesh Mehta, Anna Baez and Paul O'Loughlin - The International Ecotourism Society

12. Linking Green Productivity to Ecotourism by Asian Productivity Organisation

13. Community Based Ecotourism & Conservation in the Pacific Islands by South Pacific Biodiversity Conservation Programme

14. Best Practice Ecotourism in Queensland by Tourism Queensland

15. Best Practice Ecotourism – A Guide to Energy and Waste Minimisation by Tourism Queensland

16. Ecotourism: The Potentials and Pitfalls by Elizabeth Boo/WWF Vol.1 & 2

17. Sustainable Development of Ecotourism: A compilation of Good Practices in SMEs by WTO, 2003 Edition

18. Policies For Maximising Nature Tourism's Ecological and Economic Benefits by World Resources Institute

19. The Business of Ecotourism by Carol Patterson

20. Ecotourism and Sustainable Development: Who Owns Paradise? by Martha Honey

21. Ecotourism and Certification: Setting Standards in Practice by Martha Honey

22. The Business of Ecolodges by Ed Sanders and Elizabeth Halpenny